Troubleshooting
Windows 7

Robert Penfold

Bernard Babani (publishing) Ltd
The Grampians
Shepherds Bush Road
London W6 7NF
England

Please note

Although every care has been taken with the production of this book to ensure that any projects, designs, modifications, and/or programs, etc., contained herewith, operate in a correct and safe manner and also that any components specified are normally available in Great Britain, the Publisher and Author do not accept responsibility in any way for the failure (including fault in design) of any projects, design, modification, or program to work correctly or to cause damage to any equipment that it may be connected to or used in conjunction with, or in respect of any other damage or injury that may be caused, nor do the Publishers accept responsibility in any way for the failure to obtain specified components.

Notice is also given that if any equipment that is still under warranty is modified in any way or used or connected with home-built equipment then that warranty may be void.

© 2010 BERNARD BABANI (publishing) LTD

First Published - April 2010

British Library Cataloguing in Publication Data
A catalogue record for this book is available from the British Library

ISBN   978 0 85934 713 6

Cover Design by Gregor A
Printed and bound in Grea

Although the Windows operating systems are widely regarded as having a lack of stability, this reputation is not entirely fair. Software as complex as any version of Windows is never likely to be fully debugged, but it is not really any built-in bugs that are the major problem with Windows. It is the alterations that are made to the operating system after the basic installation process has been completed. The operating system is added to and altered each time any hardware or major piece of software is added or removed. Windows can be used with an enormous range of software and hardware, but this leaves it vulnerable to problems that originate in hardware drivers, installation programs, and uninstallers. Applications programs can also introduce difficulties if they do not strictly abide by the rules involving memory management, file naming, etc.

Windows XP was more robust than earlier versions of the operating system such as Windows ME, and it was designed to do a good job of defending itself against incompatible drivers and applications software. Windows 7 does an even better job of guarding itself against damage, but it is still not immune to problems. It is doubtful if an operating system can ever be made totally "bomb proof". In order to be usable an operating system must be flexible, but this flexibility inevitably leaves it vulnerable to problems.

Ideally the user would install Windows 7 and some applications programs, and then make no further changes to the system. For most users this is not practical though, and new hardware has to be added, software upgrades have to be installed from time to time, and so on. Most modern PCs tend to evolve over a period of time, and the operating system has to change to accommodate this evolution. If Windows 7 should cease working it is not usually too difficult to get it up and running again. Most faults introduced into the system are easily reversed, provided you know how. This book details some simple procedures that enable most Windows 7 faults to be quickly pinpointed and rectified. You do not have to be a computer expert in order to follow these procedures, but you do have to be familiar with the basics of using the Windows 7 user interface.

Where a Windows 7 installation becomes seriously damaged it may not be practical to repair it. Even if numerous files have been corrupted or deleted it is probably possible to repair the installation given enough time, but the more sensible approach is to reinstall the operating system.

Ideally this should be done by having a backup of the system and data files that can be quickly restored to the hard disc. Windows 7 has built-in backup software that make this task easy, as described in Chapter 2. No matter how badly the operating system and other files are damaged, this method soon has everything working normally again. The alternative is to reinstall everything from scratch. This is effectively what is done when upgrading from Windows XP, and the fresh install procedure is covered in Chapter 1.

Robert Penfold

Trademarks

Contents

Please note

Undertaking tasks such as changing video settings of your computer, deleting unwanted files, uninstalling software, and defragmenting a hard disc drive should not invalidate the manufacturer's warranty. Neither should using software that helps with general maintenance of the computer, such as tuning utilities and diagnostics software. Directly tinkering with the operating system, such as making changes to the Windows Registry should not normally invalidate any warranties, and should not damage the hardware. However, it could render the operating system unusable, leaving the computer out of commission. It would then be the responsibility of the user to restore the operating system to a usable state. Making direct changes to the Windows Registry is a topic that is not covered in this book, and it is something that should only be undertaken by those with the necessary experience and knowledge to sort out any problems that arise.

Adding new hardware inside a PC, such as adding memory modules, does often invalidate the manufacturer's warranty. It does not affect your statutory rights though, provided any additions made to the computer do not cause any damage. Changing settings so that the hardware operates beyond its normal parameters (over-clocking) can damage the hardware, will almost certainly invalidate the computer manufacturer's guarantee, and probably leave you very much on your own if things go awry. Over-clocking is not a subject that is included in this book.

Further, you are advised to check the Terms and Conditions of your own particular hardware and software warranties and, also, those of any equipment maintenance agreements that you might have.

Upgrading from XP and Vista

Out with the old…

Upgrading from Windows 3.1 to Windows 95 was a big step for those who made the change. A switch was being made from a 16-bit operating system to a 32-bit type. Changing from Windows 95, 98, or ME to Windows XP was another big step, and many consider that it is actually a larger change than moving from 16-bit Windows to the 32-bit variety. Matters are more straightforward for those upgrading to Windows 7 from Vista. Windows Vista and 7 are very similar, and I suppose that they are not actually all that different to their predecessor, Windows XP. So is there any point in upgrading?

The upgrade version of Windows 7 can be used with a computer running Windows Vista or XP, but upgrading from an earlier version is not possible. It is likely that a computer running an earlier version of Windows such as ME would not be able to run Windows 7, so this is probably of academic importance. In general, upgrading from Vista to Windows 7 should be very straightforward, but an upgrade from Windows XP is potentially a more problematic process. A typical computer running under Windows XP has a more basic specification than a typical PC that uses Vista. Also, an XP based computer is likely to be running older software that might not be fully compatible with Windows 7. We will consider an upgrade from Vista first.

Upgrading from Vista

The arrival of Windows Vista was not exactly greeted with universal acclaim, and it is presumably for this reason that Windows Vista was relatively short-lived. Windows 7 was designed to improve the features of Windows Vista that many felt to be inadequate in some way. Upgrading to Windows 7 is an obvious choice if you are a Vista user, and one of the many people who are dissatisfied with this version of Windows.

Upgrading is probably not an automatic choice if you are a reasonably happy user of Windows Vista, but there are some advantages to the new version of the operating system, and it is worth considering these rather than simply dismissing Windows 7 as an unnecessary upgrade. It is generally more streamlined, faster, and has a better so-called "look and feel". It is faster in the sense that it will usually take significantly less time to boot-up and shut down. Also, some application programs might run a bit faster than when using Vista, but do not expect a massive improvement in this respect.

Windows 7 is more streamlined in that it takes fewer dialogue boxes, new windows, warning messages, or whatever in order to complete many tasks. As a very simple example, in order to switch off the computer it is merely necessary to go to the Start menu and operate the Shutdown button. I suppose there is a downside to this, which is that fewer warning messages make it easier to do something that you did not intend to do. However, the warning messages associated with security matters have been retained, as have any that pop up when you are about to do something drastic that could be difficult to reverse. The Windows 7 version of UAC (user account control) still manages to do its job properly while being somewhat less irksome than the Vista version.

Vista suffered from a problem that is often referred to as software "bloat". In other words, there was just too much of it, with extra programs that most users would probably never need or use. Windows 7 has been reduced in this respect, although most of the extra software included in Vista can be downloaded free by Windows 7 users. They are available as part of Microsoft's Windows Live Essentials feature, which includes newer version of the video editing, photo editing, and Email programs.

Other improvements have been made, such as networking and the sharing of files and printers being simplified. The taskbar preview facility has been improved, and Windows XP compatibility is greatly improved if you use one of the more upmarket versions of Windows 7. Most users who upgrade seem to feel that Windows 7 is easier and more pleasant to use.

Minimum specification

If you buy Windows 7 already installed on a new PC there should be no problem, and the PC should have a specification that is high enough to run this operating system very well. The situation is often very different when upgrading from one version of Windows to another, since each new version of Windows tends to require more hardware resources than its predecessor. In particular, when compared to its predecessor, the minimum specification for a new version of Windows usually calls for a better processor, more memory, and greater hard disc space.

The situation is more straightforward with an upgrade from Windows Vista to Windows 7, since they are essentially the same operating system with the same kernel. Therefore, it is unlikely that a computer which runs at least reasonably well with Vista would have any problems with an upgrade to Windows 7. Hopefully, the opposite would actually be the case, with the computer operating in a faster and more streamlined manner after the upgrade.

It is important to emphasise that this only applies to an upgrade from Vista. As discussed later in this chapter, matters are different when upgrading to Windows 7 from Windows XP. It is by no means certain that an old PC running Windows XP would have the wherewithal to run Windows 7, so it would be essential to check that your PC is up to the task before buying Windows 7. Only proceed if there is a realistic chance of obtaining good results. This is the minimum specification needed to run Windows 7:

A processor having a clock speed of 1 gigahertz or more

1 gigabyte of memory

DirectX 9 graphics device with WDDM 1.0 or higher driver

16 gigabytes of hard disc space

DVD drive

When looking at the minimum hardware requirements for any software it has to be borne in mind that the quoted specification is the absolute minimum required to run the software, and that a system of this specification might not give usable results in practice. In fact, in most cases the quoted minimum hardware requirements do not represent the lowest specification that provides a usable system. A PC having the minimum requirements will run the software, but will usually perform so badly as to be of little or no practical use.

Memory

The only large change from the minimum specification for Vista is a doubling of the required memory from 512 megabytes to one gigabyte. It is important to bear in mind that the amount of memory required is not governed by the operating system alone. Although the one gigabyte specified for Windows 7 is double the minimum recommended for Vista, the practical experience of users suggests that one gigabyte is probably a more realistic minimum for Vista as well. Most PCs sold with Vista pre-installed had a gigabyte or more of memory fitted.

A gigabyte is sufficient to run Windows 7 reasonably well, and should still be sufficient when running one or two "run of the mill" applications, but it will not be adequate when running more demanding applications such as image and video editing software. A larger amount of memory is also required when running several small application programs simultaneously. The computer must have sufficient memory to accommodate the operating system and the application programs that you will use.

Another point to bear in mind is that many computers have an integrated graphics system. In other words, the graphics circuits are on the main board rather than being provided by a separate graphics card. While it is not totally unknown for integrated graphics systems to have their own high-speed memory, it is more normal for them to share the system memory. With the integrated graphics system using (say) 256 megabytes of system memory, the available memory for the operating system and other software is reduced by 256 megabytes. Consequently, 1.5 or even two gigabytes is a more realistic minimum for a PC that has an integrated graphics system and will be used to run demanding application software.

Clock speed

The minimum processor clock speed can never be anything more than a rough guide, since a selection of PCs running at a certain clock speed will not provide the same level of performance. The overall speed of the PC is influenced by other factors, such as the type of processor in use, the chipset on the motherboard, the amount of memory, and the performance of the video card. Anyway, it is unlikely that any PC having a 1GHz processor will run Windows 7 really well, and something closer to 2GHz is a more realistic minimum.

Graphics

Any reasonably modern graphics card should be capable of running DirectX 9, but this ability can not be taken for granted with older graphics cards. It should not be too difficult to check whether the graphics system in your PC can use DirectX 9, and with most PCs this information is available from the manufacturer's web site. If your PC is already running under Vista, then it is certainly capable of using at least DirectX 9, and it will already be doing so. Note that some software, and particularly the more advanced games programs, require DirectX 10 in order to function properly. Such programs require a graphics card that goes well beyond the bare minimum capabilities needed in order to run Windows 7 properly.

Sound

In order to run Windows 7 it is not essential to have a particularly advanced sound system installed, but it is important to realise that some aspects of the more advanced versions of Windows 7 can only be used with a computer that does have an upmarket soundcard. Actually, in order to fully utilise some aspects of Windows 7 it is necessary to have other media equipment installed such as a television card and a remote control system. Using an advanced version of this operating system will not turn a "run of the mill" PC into a top quality media type. The PC must have a suitably high specification, including any special hardware that is required by some functions. If you have a "bells and whistles" PC that runs properly under Vista, it should continue to do so with Windows 7.

Realistic minimum

In order to run Windows 7 reasonably well the minimum specification is therefore something like this:

Processor having a clock speed of 2GHz or more

1GB of memory, but preferably 2GB or more

Large hard disc drive (80GB or more)

Modern video system capable of using DirectX 9.0 and a resolution of at least 1024 by 768 pixels

DVD drive

Mouse or other Windows compatible pointing device

Any reasonably modern soundcard or integrated sound facility

If required, additional media components such as a television card or an upmarket video and audio system

Do not be surprised if you obtain poor results using Windows 7 with a system that only just meets these requirements. Even with a somewhat higher specification it is possible that some aspects of performance might not be very good. On the other hand, your PC should run well enough under Windows 7 when using most application software provided it has a reasonably fast processor and a reasonably large amount of memory installed.

XP upgrade

Computers that run under Windows XP vary from fairly modern and powerful PCs that are easily capable of running Windows 7 to very old PCs that originally ran under Windows ME and were upgraded to XP. The minimum processor speed for XP is 233 megahertz, with 300 megahertz or more recommended. However, even with a fairly old PC it is unlikely that Windows 7's one gigahertz minimum requirement for the processor will not be met. Bear in mind though, that an old processor running at one or two gigahertz will probably provide less than a tenth of the processing speed of a modern two or three gigahertz chip. Consequently, an old processor that has a clock rate well above the minimum requirement might not run Windows 7 particularly well, but results should be perfectly acceptable.

Memory and hard disc space are more likely causes of problems. Believe it or not, Windows XP could run after a fashion using 64 megabytes of memory, and the recommended minimum for full operation was just 128 megabytes. Most XP systems actually have two or four times the recommended minimum, but even 512 megabytes is insufficient for Windows 7. Many PCs running under XP will therefore need their memory upgraded to at least one gigabyte before they can be upgraded to Windows 7.

The hard disc requirements for Windows XP are similarly modest, with 1.5 gigabytes being needed for a typical installation. This is less than a tenth of the disc space required for a normal Windows 7 installation. A PC that has a 20 to 30 gigabyte hard disc drive is probably not a realistic candidate for a Windows 7 installation. Remember that 16 gigabytes is the disc space needed for the Windows installation, and that further hard disc space is required for temporary storage, applications software, and your data. A 40 gigabyte drive is a realistic minimum for a Windows 7 installation. No doubt most PCs running XP actually meet this requirement, and are therefore suitable for an upgrade provided at least 20 gigabytes of free hard disc space can be provided. More than the basic 16 gigabytes for the Windows installation is needed, since a few gigabytes will be needed to provide Windows with temporary storage space.

Fig.1.1 The Upgrade Advisor program can be downloaded from the Microsoft web site

The video card is perhaps the most likely cause of problems, since Windows XP itself requires nothing more than a fairly basic VGA video card with a resolution of 800 by 600 pixels. Obviously some software requires something more potent, and many PCs running Windows XP have a fairly powerful video system. It might still be inadequate to run Windows 7, with its need for a card running at least DirectX 9.0 in order to provide its fancy effects. Upgrading the video card might not be very expensive, but it can be difficult to find a modern video card that will fit the expansion slots used on older PCs.

A final point to bear in mind is that it is probably not worthwhile upgrading a PC that is nearing the end of its useful life. This is not really a cost effective way of doing things, since it would mean abandoning the Windows upgrade and any new hardware for the upgrade after a year or so or perhaps even less. It is generally better to carry on with the old hardware and operating system for as long as is reasonably possible, and then buy a new PC that will presumably come complete with a preinstalled copy of Windows 7.

Checking

If in doubt, it is possible to run a program that will check whether your PC is suitable for an upgrade to Windows 7. This program is actually

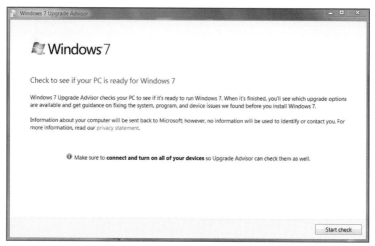

Fig.1.2 This window provides some useful information

part of the Windows 7 installation program. The suitability of the PC is checked as part of the normal upgrade process. The purpose of this routine is to warn you of any potential problems with the hardware and the installed software.

The standalone version of the advisor program is useful if you wish to upgrade, but would like to check the suitability of your PC before buying the upgrade software. It will probably be made available on a few of the "free" discs supplied with computer magazines, and it can be downloaded from the Microsoft web site at this address (Figure 1.1):

http://www.microsoft.com/downloads/
details.aspx?FamilyID=1B544E90-7659-4BD9-9E51-
2497C146AF15&displaylang=en

A small Window appears when the program is run, and you have to agree to the usual licence conditions by ticking the appropriate checkbox. Next a small information screen appears (Figure 1.2), and this explains what the program will do, and it also points out that any devices used with the PC should be connected to the appropriate ports and should be switched on. The program can only scan and check the suitability of USB hardware and other external gadgets if they are accessible to the program, so any external devices not connected to the PC or left switched off will not be checked.

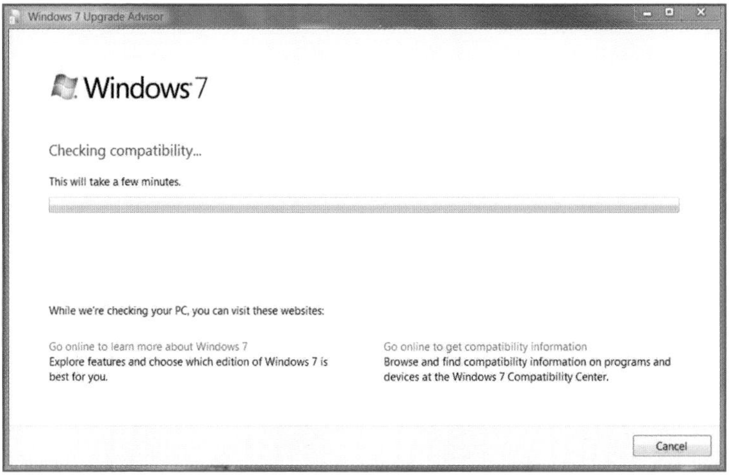

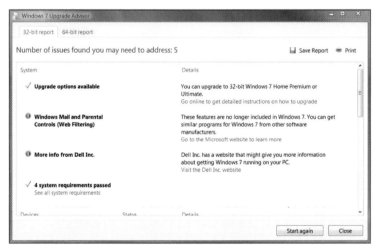

Fig.1.3 This window appears while the program makes its checks

Operating the Start Check button starts the checking process, and the window of Figure 1.3 then appears. An animated status bar indicates that the checking process is underway, but it does not give any indication of the time required for completion. The scanning process might take a

Fig.1.4 The checking process has been completed

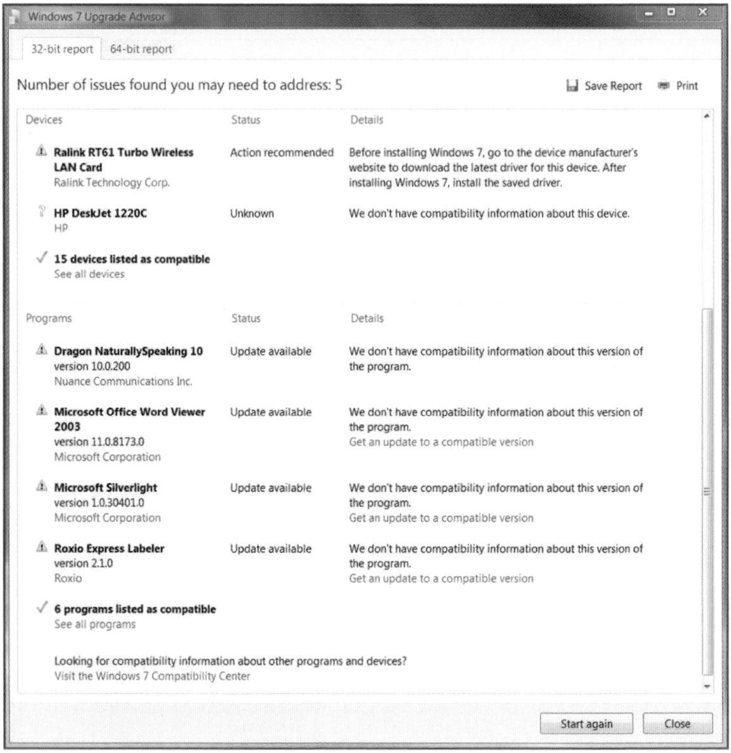

Fig.1.5 *It will probably be necessary to scroll down in order to see all the results in a long list*

few minutes, but eventually the window will change to look like Figure 1.4, confirming that the checking process has been completed.

The PC used in this example has a fair amount of hardware and software installed, and it was virtually inevitable that at least one or two potential problems would be reported by the advisor program. Do not worry if your PC produces a list of compatibility issues, because it is possible that most or all of them will be minor problems. There is a link for most entries, and activating a link produces a window that gives more details about any compatibility problems. You will probably have to scroll down the window in order to get the full list of results (Figure 1.5).

The important part of the list of test results is the one that deals with the system requirements. This is the one that details any major deficiencies in the hardware, such as too little hard disc space or a processor that is too slow. Unless you are prepared to make any necessary upgrades to the computer's hardware, there is no point in proceeding any further if a problem is indicated here.

An exception is where a lack of free hard disc space is indicated, but you are able to increase the amount of free space by uninstalling programs that are no longer used, deleting data files that are no longer needed, or whatever, in order to provide sufficient disc space for the upgrade. Bear in mind that at least a couple of gigabytes of free hard disc space will be needed in order to run Windows 7 efficiently once the upgrade has been completed, so you actually need somewhat more free disc space than is needed in order to accommodate all the files for Windows 7.

Suitable versions

The first section of the test results indicates the upgrade version or versions of Windows 7 that can be used. As far as I can gather, it is only possible to upgrade to a version of Windows 7 that is roughly equivalent to the version of Vista already installed, or in some cases an upgrade to a more advanced version of Windows 7 is possible. An upgrade from an advanced version of Vista to a more basic version of Windows 7 is not permitted.

This might simply be due to a Microsoft marketing policy, or there could be technical reasons for these upgrade restrictions. Either way, if you buy an inappropriate upgrade product it will not be possible to install it on your PC. Therefore, make a note of the upgrade version or versions mentioned in the test results, and only buy a compatible upgrade product. It is perhaps worth mentioning that it is not usually possible to upgrade Microsoft software using a full retail product. If you obtain a full version of Windows 7 it will almost certainly be necessary to install it from scratch.

There will be one or two information sections near the top of the list of results. One of these simply explains that Windows Mail and the Parental Control web filtering are not available in Windows 7, but that similar facilities can be obtained using programs from other software producers. There will probably be another section suggesting that you contact the maker of your PC for information about any Windows 7 upgrades that they can supply. However, it should not be necessary to obtain an upgrade from the producer of the PC, and an appropriate upgrade product from a software vendor should work equally well.

Driver problems

Scrolling down the list of problems will probably reveal some that are software related. These really fall into two categories, which are driver problems and those associated with application programs. These are listed separately in the Devices and Programs sections respectively. In this example there are 15 devices that are fully compatible and two where there are potential problems.

One of the problem devices is a wi-fi card that needs a more up-to-date driver program. The suggested solution is to download the newest versions of the driver from the hardware manufacturer's web site, store it on the hard disc, and install it once the upgrade to Windows 7 has been completed. I did download the latest version of the driver, but it proved to be unnecessary.

The other problem device is an inkjet printer that is "not as young as it used to be". The Upgrade Advisor software has failed to recognise it, and can offer no assistance. However, the printer manufacturer's web site indicated that a basic driver for the printer could be obtained using the Windows Update facility of Windows 7, so the printer would actually be usable after the upgrade, but some features of the original driver software might not be available. This proved to be another non-problem, and Windows automatically installed a driver that worked exactly the same as the Vista version.

I have sometimes seen it claimed that Vista drivers will always work properly with Windows 7. This claim is based on the fact that both operating systems are based on the same kernel, and a driver that works with one should also work with the other. Unfortunately, in practice it is not always as simple as that, and some Vista drivers do not work properly with Windows 7. This is most likely to occur where a driver includes some form of user interface, rather than simply running unseen in the background. Anyway, the fact that a driver works properly with Vista by no means guarantees that it will also perform flawlessly with Windows 7.

Troublesome software

All the remaining problems listed in this example are potential problems with application programs. It is unlikely that there will be any major problems in this respect with a computer that is running under Vista. It might be necessary to install a few software updates in order to ensure perfect results, but it is unlikely that it will be necessary to buy any major software upgrades. The web sites of the relevant manufacturers should have the information you require, together with any necessary updates.

It should be noted that there are some types of software that only work properly if they are used with a suitable version of Windows, and that there could be severe damage to the operating system if they are used with the wrong version. It is mainly security software that falls into this category, such as antivirus and anti spyware programs, plus some utility programs such as those designed to find and fix hard disc problems. Do not use any software of these types unless the manufacturer specifically states that it is suitable for operation with Windows 7.

If the Upgrade Advisor indicates that an item of software must be uninstalled prior to the upgrade, then it is essential to do so. Do not be tempted to try the program to see what happens. Anyway, the upgrade program will probably refuse to go ahead with the upgrade if it detects a serious problem, including an inappropriate program installed on the system.

Serious problems with application programs are far more likely when upgrading from Windows XP. In particular, the types of software just mentioned are unlikely to work after the upgrade unless newer versions are obtained, but there are other types of program that refuse to work properly after an upgrade to Windows 7. Some of these problems are not serious and do not render the software unusable. Others can be avoided by using the compatibility modes of Windows 7. However, it might be necessary to buy upgrades to some items of software, and where appropriate, this additional cost must be taken into account when deciding whether to go ahead with the upgrade.

Upgrade decision

It is unlikely that there will be any major hardware problems provided your PC uses "run of the mill" hardware that is reasonably up to date. There will not always be Windows 7 support for older hardware. It is unlikely that driver software for an old version of Windows will be usable with Windows 7, which would probably refuse to install old driver software. Vista drivers are sometimes suitable, which I suppose is not surprising given that both operating systems are based on the same kernel. If essential but out-of-date hardware is found to be totally incompatible with Windows 7, then it is a matter of "biting the bullet" and not going ahead with the upgrade, or upgrading any unsupported hardware first.

If only one inexpensive item of hardware has to be replaced, it should certainly be worthwhile continuing with the upgrade. Obviously, the

Fig.1.6 The DriverGuide.com home page

upgrade might not be feasible if the PC requires expensive changes in order to accommodate Windows 7, or if there are expensive peripheral gadgets that will have to be replaced. The same is true if expensive upgrades to the application software will also be needed. This is a subjective matter and one where you have to weigh up the costs against the advantages and make your own decision.

Finding drivers

So-called generic hardware is a common cause of upgrade woes. This is either anonymous hardware that carries no manufacturer's name on the device itself or in the documentation, or the name of the manufacturer is given but is one that no one has ever heard of. The problem with this type of hardware is that there is usually no support available from the manufacturer's web site. If you are lucky, a web address will be provided somewhere in the documentation or a search engine will help you locate one. In most cases though, the level of support provided by the big name manufacturers is not available for generic hardware. There is often

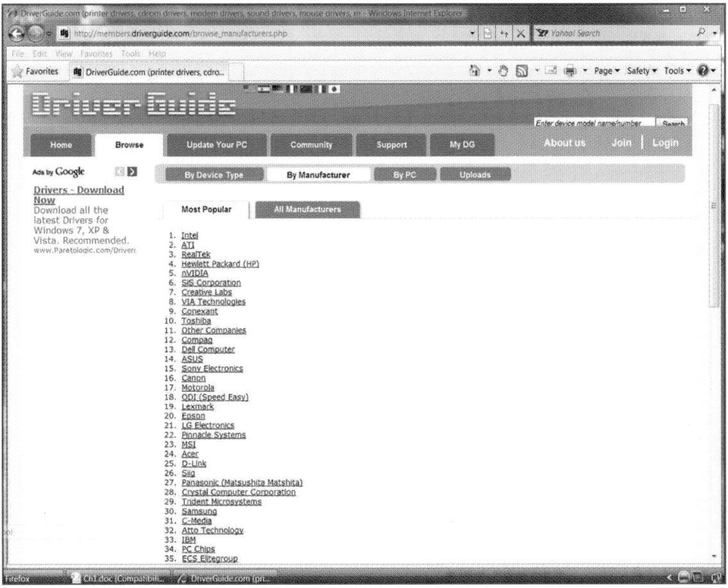

Fig.1.7 Drivers are available for products from numerous makers

no ongoing support at all for this type of hardware, which in part accounts for its low cost.

The fact that a piece of generic hardware lacks a web address for support does not necessarily mean that there is no hope of finding suitable Windows 7 drivers. However, it does mean that if the device drivers do exist, finding them will be much more difficult. With generic hardware that came as part of a PC, the Support section of the PC manufacturer's web site might have the drivers you need. A call to the PC manufacturer's help line might also produce some useful information. Provided the PC you are using is not in the "golden oldie" category, the maker should provide ongoing support for all the hardware, including any no-name hardware.

Computer chip manufacturers often produce generic driver software for their products. If your piece of problem hardware is a modem that is based on (say) a Motorola chipset, the obvious starting point is the Motorola web site. Any search engine should soon locate the chip manufacturer's web site. Unfortunately, this will not always produce a source of suitable drivers. Quite reasonably, the manufacturer of the

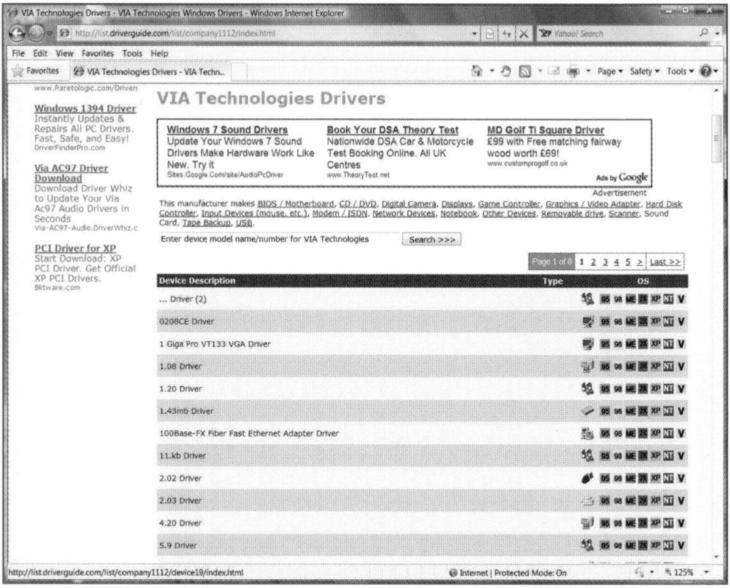

Fig.1.8 A list of drivers for devices from VIA Technologies

chips might consider that it is the job of the equipment producer to supply support for their products. However, in practice the sites of chip makers often prove helpful, and it is certainly worthwhile looking to see if there is anything useful on offer.

Driver sites

If a search of the chip manufacturer's site proves to be fruitless, other avenues can be pursued. There are plenty of sites that offer help with device drivers, and using "device drivers" as the search string in a search engine will produce a useful list of driver sites. These sites mostly offer a great deal of general information about software drivers, plus advice for beginners on installing them. In most cases there are also search facilities and advice on finding suitable driver programs.

One example of such a site is DriverGuide.com (Figure 1.6). You have to register in order to utilise this site, but registration for the basic facilities of the site is free. Amongst other things, the site includes search facilities that enable the user to search for a certain manufacturer, drivers for a

Fig.1.9 WinDrivers.com is a popular driver search engine

certain type of hardware, and so on. In Figure 1.7 a list of manufacturers has been provided, and in Figure 1.8 the available drivers for VIA Technologies has been listed.

Probably the best known site for device drivers is WinDrivers.com (Figure 1.9). This site provides a lot of general advice together with useful search facilities, including one where you search for drivers from a specific manufacturer (Figure 1.10). I have found HelpDrivers.com (Figure 1.11) very useful when tracking down drivers. The current version works on the basis of selecting a type of gadget and the manufacturer, with a list of relevant drivers then being provided (Figure 1.12).

There is no guarantee that Windows 7 drivers will be available for any awkward pieces of hardware, but if they do exist they will almost certainly be available somewhere on the Internet. Note that the new drivers must not be installed until after the upgrade to Windows 7 has been completed. Some installation programs will detect that the operating system is inappropriate for the new device drivers and will refuse to install them. Other installation programs will go ahead anyway, regardless of the consequences.

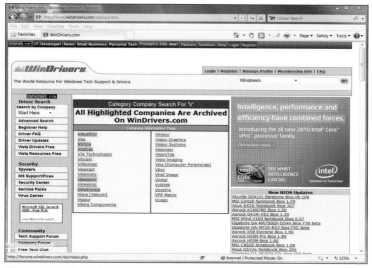

Fig.1.10 Again, drivers are available for the products from a number of manufacturers

Fig.1.11 With Help.Drivers.com you first select a type of gadget

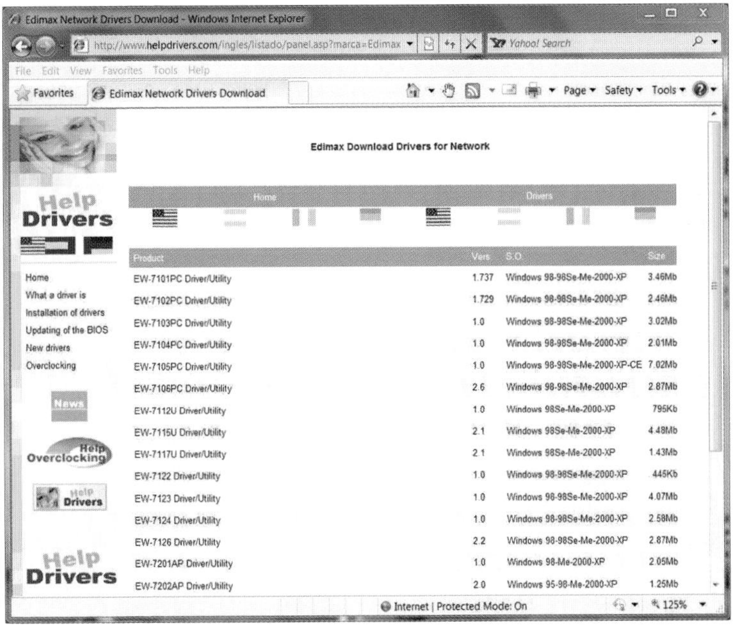

Fig.1.12 A list of drivers has been provided, based on the selected device type and manufacturer

If the new drivers are installed in the existing version of Windows, it is virtually certain that the relevant hardware will cease to work properly. It is also quite possible that the existing Windows installation will be damaged to the point where it fails to boot correctly. Of course, the obvious exception to all this is where drivers are specified as suitable for the old and new versions of the operating system, but it is still advisable to install the Windows upgrade first and then update the drivers.

Never try to upgrade any Windows installation that has a serious fault. People sometimes try to fix a faulty Windows installation by upgrading to the latest version, but the chances of this ploy succeeding are minimal. The upgrade program might detect the problem and refuse to continue. If an upgrade on a faulty Windows installation is allowed to go ahead, the most likely outcome is that things will come to an abrupt halt somewhere during the upgrade. It can then be very difficult indeed to sort things out. In most cases Windows has to be installed from scratch, and this process is not something that should be taken lightly.

Fig.1.13 The standard version of the Windows Control Panel

Uninstalling hardware

In general, where new device drivers will be needed after the upgrade, there is no need to remove any hardware or drivers before upgrading to Windows 7. It is better to complete the upgrade first and then install the new device drivers. The presence of the old drivers or the hardware itself should not hinder the upgrade in any way. Installing new drivers effectively removes the old ones, thus ensuring that the old drivers will not adversely affect the new installation.

It is not strictly necessary to remove any hardware that is not supported by Windows 7, and will not be used once the PC has been upgraded. However, there is little point in leaving an expansion card in place if it will not be used any more, and uninstalling it makes quite sure that it cannot hinder the upgrade. It also makes sure that the card does not make any unnecessary use of the computer's resources.

It is advisable to uninstall the device drivers before physically removing an expansion card. First, go to the Windows Control Panel by selecting the Control Panel option from the Start menu. This produces a window like the one of Figure 1.13. Left-click the Classic View link near the top left-hand corner of the window, which will change the window to look

Fig.1.14 Here the Control Panel has been switched to the Classic version. Scroll down to reveal the System icon

Fig.1.15 The System Properties window

Fig.1.16 Device Manager lists all the installed hardware

something like Figure 1.14. If necessary, scroll the window downward to reveal the System icon, and then double-click this icon. Note that the entries in Control Panel vary somewhat from one PC to another, but the System icon should always be present.

Double-clicking the System icon produces a new window like the one of Figure 1.15. This is the System Properties window, and it defaults to the General section that gives some basic information about the PC. Next operate the Device Manager link, which launches the Device Manager program in a new window (Figure 1.16).

The Device Manager window lists the various hardware categories that cover most of the PC's internal hardware, and it will probably include some external peripheral devices. One of these categories should contain the hardware you wish to uninstall, and double-clicking the appropriate icon will expand that category to show the individual items it contains. In the example of Figure 1.16 the "Sound, video and game controllers" entry has been expanded, and it contains two items.

In order to uninstall an item of hardware, double-click its entry to launch its properties window, and then operate the Driver tab near the top of the window. The new version of the window (Figure 1.17) has an Uninstall

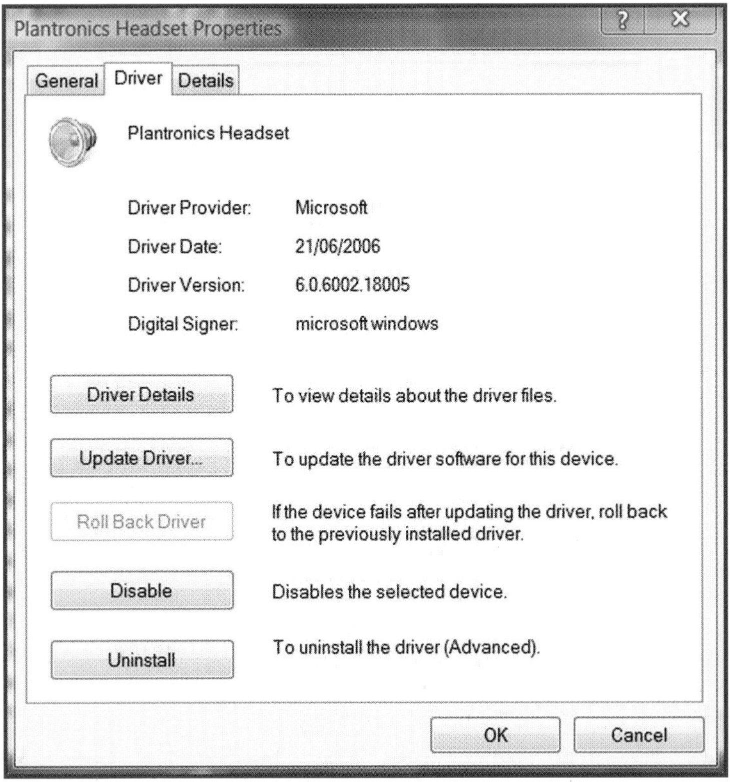

Fig.1.17 Use the Uninstall button to remove the driver from the system

button, and operating this produces a warning message like the one of Figure 1.18. Left-click the OK button to proceed and remove the drivers for the selected piece of hardware. The appropriate entry in Device Manager should then disappear. If the uninstalled hardware was the only device in its category, the entry for that category will also be removed. Note that it is not possible to select and then remove a category. The entry for a category can only be removed by individually uninstalling each piece of hardware it contains.

Note that some pieces of hardware perform more than one function and therefore have multiple entries in Device Manager. An audio card for example, often provides a MIDI interface and possibly a games port in addition to various audio functions. Consequently, a typical audio card

has three or four device drivers listed in Device Manager. I have encountered some that had five or six device drivers listed in Device Manager. All the relevant drivers should be removed when uninstalling any multifunction devices.

Fig.1.18 Operate the OK button to continue

Physically uninstalling

With the device drivers uninstalled, it is likely that the computer will try to reinstall the hardware the next time it is booted into Windows unless the hardware is removed from the PC. Shut down Windows and switch off the computer at the mains supply before doing any work on the computer. Modern desktop PC cases are mostly of the ATX variety, and with these it is only necessary to remove the left-hand side panel in order to gain access to the expansion cards. With ATX cases each panel is normally held in place by two or three screws, which are again situated at the rear of the unit.

There are usually other fixing screws at the rear of a PC, holding in place things like the power supply and subassemblies of the case. Look at the way everything fits together and be careful to remove the correct screws. Note that some PCs have fancy cases that can be difficult to open. However, if you study the case for a while it should be possible to "crack" the problem. The PC's instruction should give some guidance on gaining access to the interior of the case and adding or removing expansion cards.

Each expansion card has a metal bracket (Figure 1.19) that is bolted to the rear of the PC's chassis. With this bolt removed it not usually too difficult to pull the card free of its expansion slot, but it can require a fair amount of force to remove a card that has been in place for some time. Pull steadily on the card using no more force than is absolutely necessary to pull it free. Do not use brute force if the card is difficult to remove. A rocking action will usually loosen an awkward card so that it can be pulled free without having to use excessive force.

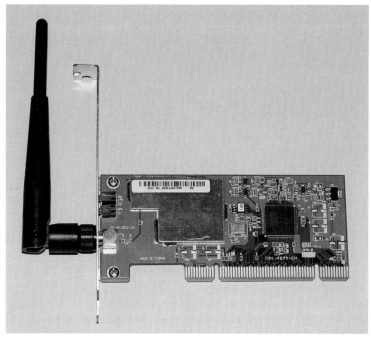

Fig.1.19 This wi-fi card has the usual mounting bracket. It is on the left near the antenna

There are three types of expansion slot in common use today, which are the standard PC1 type, PCI Express 1X, and the PCI Express 16X (Figure 1.20). Most expansion cards are of the standard PCI variety, but PCI Express 1X cards are gaining in popularity. The 16X version of the PCI Express slot is primarily intended for video cards, and this type of slot has a simple locking mechanism at the front that must be unlocked before trying to remove the card. The older AGP expansion slot also has a simple locking mechanism at the front.

If your PC was supplied with some spare blanking plates, one of these can be bolted in the position formerly occupied by the mounting bracket of the expansion card. It does not matter too much if you do not have a spare blanking plate, and omitting it might improve ventilation and help to keep the computer cool! Some of these plates clip in place and do not require the mounting bolt. These are easy to spot, because the top section is not flat, but instead has a curved section that is used to clip it in place.

Fig.1.20   Three types of expansion card slot. The blue one near the middle is a PCI Express 16X type for a video card

With the card removed and the blanking plate in position, fit the outer casing and boot the computer into Windows. Once Windows has loaded, go to Device Manager and check that the entry for the deleted device driver has not reappeared. If necessary, remove the device driver's entry again, reboot Windows, and then look for the entry once more. You have probably deleted the wrong device driver if it keeps reappearing! The hardware for the driver is still present in the PC, so the Plug and Play system reinstalls the driver each time the computer is booted into Windows. With the hardware removed from the computer, the entry for the correct driver should be easy to spot. It will probably be marked with a yellow exclamation mark.

Uninstalling software

If it is necessary to remove any software prior to upgrading it is essential that it is uninstalled properly, rather than simply obliterating any folders that contain the files for the program that you wish to remove. Deleting folders that contain programs and support files is a good way to make Windows unstable, and can even prevent it from booting properly. It could certainly produce more problems than it solves when trying to upgrade Windows.

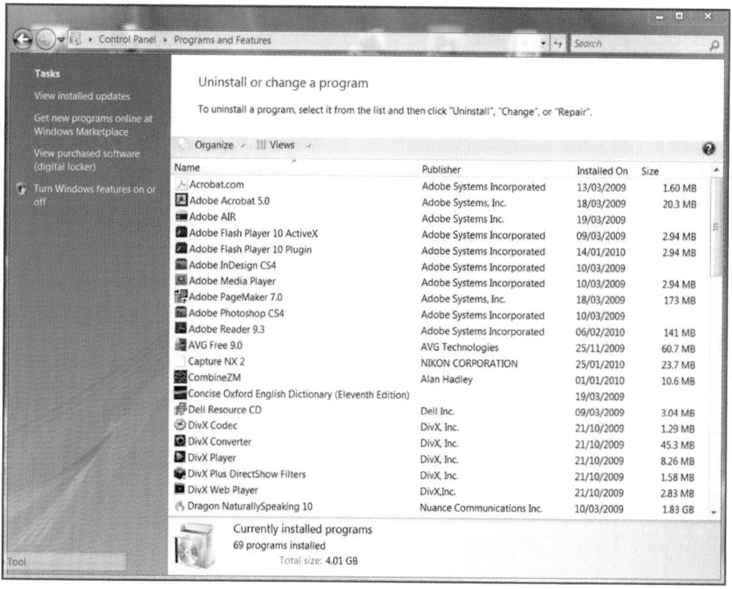

Fig.1.21 All the installed programs are listed here

Most programs can be removed using the built-in facilities of Windows. To remove software via this route, go to the Classic version of the Windows Control Panel and double-click the icon labelled Add/Remove Programs (Windows XP) or Programs and Features (Windows Vista). This produces the appropriate window (Figure 1.21), where the program you wish to remove should be listed. Left-click on its entry in the list to select the correct program, and then with Windows XP operate the Change/Remove button or the Remove button, as appropriate. With Windows Vista the appropriate entry is again selected, after which the Uninstall button near the top of the Windows is operated.

The removal process is customised to suit the particular program being uninstalled, so there is some variation from one program to another. Things should be very straightforward, but the user normally has to provide some further input, even if it is only to confirm that the uninstall process should be allowed to go ahead. In some cases it is possible to leave parts of a suite of programs in place while uninstalling others. In the current context it is only a complete removal of the program that will be needed. Some programs require the computer to be restarted in order to make the removal process take full effect. It is not essential to restart the computer immediately, but it is probably best to do so and check that software has been uninstalled correctly.

Registering and WPA

Registering Windows was optional prior to Windows XP, but with XP, Vista, and 7 it is not possible to use the program beyond a trial period unless you do so. Strictly speaking, it is not necessary to register Windows in order to go on using it indefinitely. It is the Windows Product Activation (WPA) that is essential, but this is normally done as part of the registration process. In effect, the Windows 7 installation DVD contains a fully working 30-day demonstration version of the operating system. If you ignore the onscreen warning messages and do not go through the WPA/registration process, the operating system will refuse to boot properly, or it will boot into a version of Windows that has greatly restricted facilities. All is not lost if you reach this stage, because it is still possible to go through the WPA/registration process and get the operating system fully working again

Anti-piracy

Windows Product Activation was, to say the least, a bit controversial when it was introduced with Windows XP. The idea is to prevent casual piracy of the operating system. However, like most anti-piracy systems, it does not make life any easier for legitimate users of the product. It can make life very much more difficult for legitimate users, although it will not necessarily do so. As pointed out previously, the program on the disc when you buy Windows 7 is effectively just a 30-day demonstration version. Entering the product identification number during installation was sufficient to get earlier versions of Windows fully working, but with Windows XP, Vista, and 7 it is only the first step in the activation process. Entering this number during installation gets Windows ready for activation, but it does not actually activate it.

Where possible, it is definitely advisable to opt for automatic activation via the Internet. The telephone alternative requires you to read a 50-digit code to a Microsoft representative. This code appears onscreen during the activation process. This is bad enough, but you then have to enter a 42-digit code supplied by the representative. This is clearly an awkward and time-consuming way of doing things, and there is plenty of scope for errors to occur. By contrast, activation over the Internet is quick and there is virtually no chance of errors occurring.

With an upgrade version of Windows 7 the upgrade is being used with a PC that already has a legitimate version of Windows XP or Vista installed, and the existing Windows installation will have been activated already. However, it is still necessary to activate the Windows 7 upgrade, which as far as the activation process is concerned, is treated much the same as if it was being installed from scratch. The activation of the original installation seems to be of no importance once the upgraded installation has been activated.

Some versions of Windows do not use product activation, and these are mainly the preinstalled copies from the larger PC manufacturers, and the preinstalled copies on PCs sold to large organisations. Even where no product activation was required originally, it will still be needed when using an ordinary upgrade version of Windows 7. It is also needed when using an OEM (original equipment manufacturer) version, which is essentially the same as the retail version, but is supplied with a new PC. Note that it is unlikely that the upgrade process will be possible unless the original installation is legitimate and it has been activated properly. Trying to upgrade a "cracked" copy of Windows that does not have program activation is almost certain to fail.

WPA problems

Having to go through the WPA process should be no more than a minor inconvenience, and it is not the necessity for activation that is the main "bone of contention". The activation key is derived from your Windows product identification number and the hardware installed in the PC. To be more precise, it is typically these items of hardware that are used to produce the number:

Microprocessor type

Microprocessor serial number

Display adapter

SCSI adapter (if fitted)

IDE adapter

Network adapter (if fitted)

RAM amount

Hard drive

Hard drive volume serial number

CD/DVD drives

When Windows XP/Vista/7 is booted, as part of the boot-up process the installed hardware is checked. The boot process is only completed if the installed hardware matches the full product key that is stored on the hard disc drive during the activation process. On the face of it, two computers having identical hardware could use the same activation key. In practice, this is not possible because the network adapter and processor serial numbers are unique. Two seemingly identical PCs would actually need different activation keys due to the processors and (where appropriate) the network card having different serial numbers.

There is a potential problem, in that any changes to the hardware will cause a mismatch during the checking process at boot-up. This problem is not as great as it might seem, because you are allowed a certain amount of leeway. Up to four of the items of hardware listed previously can be altered without the need to reactivate the operating system. If more than four items are changed, the activation mechanism will probably assume that the system has been copied to another computer, and it will halt the boot process.

This does not mean that you will have to buy Windows again. It will be necessary to call the WPA clearinghouse though, in order to obtain a new activation key. Frequent changes to the computer's hardware and calls to the WPA centre would presumably result in Microsoft refusing to provide further activation codes. You are permitted four changes to the hardware in 120 days or less. This suggests that you can make as many changes to the hardware as you like provided they are made slowly so that there are no more than four changes in each 120 day period. I have not tested this in practice though.

There is little likelihood of problems unless you undertake a massive hardware upgrade. A call to the WPA centre should then get things working again. However, it is best not to be too eager to activate a newly installed copy of Windows 7. This is especially important when upgrading from an earlier version of Windows if you are unsure about the compatibility of some pieces of hardware. You are given the opportunity to go through the activation process once the upgrade has been completed, but it is best not to do so at this stage. First, load any new drivers that are required, and try out the new system. If necessary, upgrade some of the hardware, and only go through the activation process when everything is working properly. You have 30 days to get everything working properly, which should be more than ample.

It is not necessary to wait for the 30 days to expire before activating Windows 7. The activation process can be started at any time by going

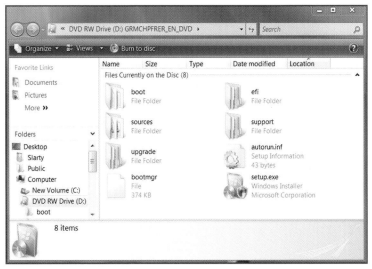

Fig.1.22 Double-click the Setup.exe icon

to the Start menu and launching the Control Panel. Activate the System and Security link, and then the System link in the new version of the window. This produces a window that provides some basic information about the computer, and near the bottom it will indicate the number of days left before the trial period expires and activation becomes essential. There will also be a link here that initiates the activation process.

32 or 64-bit?

Recent versions of Windows have been made available in 32-bit and 64-bit editions. Most modern PCs are capable of running 64-bit versions of Windows, but the 32-bit option remains the standard choice for most users. Windows 7 is not sold as separate 32-bit and 64-bit versions. Whether you buy a full retail copy or an upgrade version, it will contain separate 32-bit and 64-bit installation DVDs. Of course, you can only use one disc or the other, and not both. Only one product key is provided, so it is only possible to activate and use one copy of Windows.

It is essential to use the right installation DVD when upgrading Windows. If you are not sure whether your PC is currently running a 32-bit or 64-bit version of Windows, it is easy to find out. This information is provided by

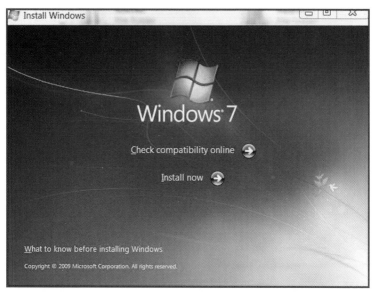

Fig.1.23 Left-click the Install Now button if you are ready to proceed

the information screen of Figure 1.15. It should also be provided by the Upgrade Advisor program in the results section that deals with the upgrade versions that are suitable for your PC.

Getting started

Note that with Windows 7 you do not upgrade a Vista or an XP installation by booting from the upgrade installation disc. Booting from the installation DVD is the method used when installing Windows on a new PC with a hard disc that has not been formatted or partitioned, but it is not used when upgrading. The only way to upgrade to Windows 7 is to first go into Windows XP or Vista, which must be a legitimate installation, and then insert the Windows 7 installation disc into a DVD drive. The disc will probably not autorun, so you have to use the "Run Setup.exe" option when the usual pop-up window appears. Alternatively, use the "Open folder and view files" option, and when the window shown in Figure 1.22 appears, double-click the Setup.exe icon. Either way, the new window of Figure 1.23 will be displayed.

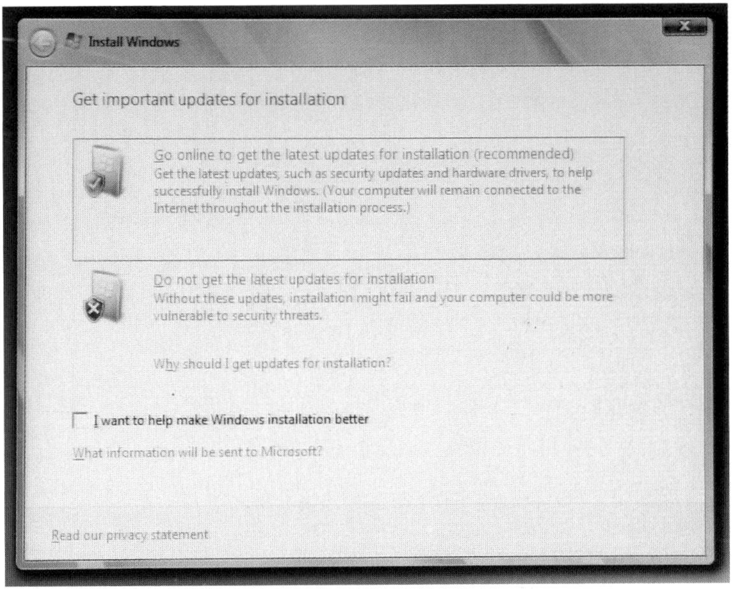

Fig.1.24 By default any available online updates will be used. I opted
         not to use this facility

A number of options are available from this window, including one to go
online and check the compatibility of your PC. You should really have
done this already, in addition to carrying out any recommendations. If
no compatibility check has been made previously, then you should
certainly go through this process now. Provided the necessary checks
and amendments to the system and hardware have been made, operate
the Install Now button to proceed with the upgrade.

Vista upgrade

After a delay while temporary files are copied to the hard disc drive, the
window of Figure 1.24 is produced. This offers the choice of installing
Windows 7 using the version on the DVD, or going online to get any
available updates. It probably makes little difference whether you opt to
install an updated version, or to install the original version and then update
it later. The final installation is presumably the same either way, and the
time taken is probably much the same.

Of course, it is only possible to use the online updates option if the
computer has an active Internet connection, and this really needs to be

some form of broadband connection. For this example I opted to install Windows 7 without going online for the latest updates. You should tick the checkbox if you would like the installation program to provide feedback to Microsoft that will help with the production of future products.

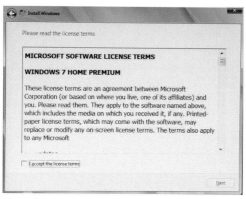

Again, using this option requires an active Internet connection.

Before the upgrade can proceed you must agree to the licence terms (Figure 1.25). This moves things on to the window of Figure 1.26, which offers a choice of a standard upgrade or a custom type. The standard type is used when upgrading Windows

Fig.1.25 Agree to the licence conditions to continue

Vista, and as far as possible it retains your current settings and application program installations. It also leaves all your data files intact. In other words, the upgrade leaves Windows and the computer in general much as it was before the upgrade, but you will be running Windows 7 instead of Vista. Being realistic about matters, it will probably be necessary to undertake a few manual changes in order to get everything working to your satisfaction, but nothing more than this should be needed.

The custom upgrade option is used if you need to install Windows 7 from scratch. Since this effectively wipes the hard disc of all your programs as well as the existing Windows installation, it is an option that should not be used unless there is a good reason for doing so. With a Vista upgrade it is unlikely that there will be a good reason for using a custom installation. It might be the way to go if the existing installation is badly damaged and there seems to be little chance of repairing it. As pointed out previously, trying to upgrade a damaged Windows installation has little chance of success.

It might also be worth using this type of upgrade if the existing installation has become "bloated", and is running in a slow and inefficient manner. However, the main reason for using the custom option, and the reason it is included at all, is that it is the only method available when upgrading

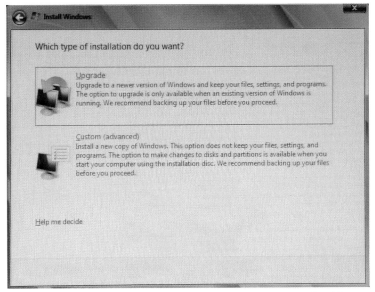

Fig.1.26 The Upgrade option is normally used when upgrading Vista

Windows XP. Upgrading Windows XP using the custom option is covered later in this chapter, and the relevant sections should be consulted if you intend to use this method for any reason.

Problems

Assuming the standard upgrade method will be used, the next window (Figure 1.27) provides details of any problems that must be resolved before proceeding. Sometimes it is necessary to exit the Setup program and reboot the computer

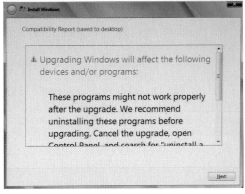

Fig.1.27 Detected problems are listed here

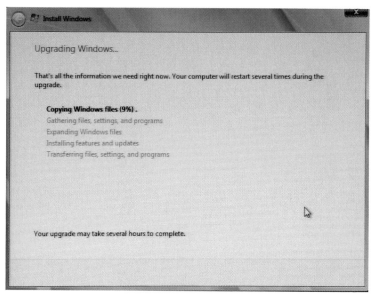

Fig.1.28 The upgrade process is under way

so that certain files can take effect. More usually, there will be one or more programs installed that must be uninstalled before going ahead with the upgrade. In this example the Setup program indicated that there was one program that needed to be uninstalled. This usually means exiting the Setup program, uninstalling the program in the usual way, and then starting the Setup program again.

In this case the program in question had already been removed, so I opted to carry straight on to the next window (Figure 1.28). This is where the Windows upgrade starts in earnest, and things will progress in a largely automatic process for some time. Do not expect the upgrade to be quick. The typical time for an upgrade seems to be two hours or so, and it could take much longer than this. The computer will probably reboot itself at least a couple of times before the basic installation process is completed. The small windows show how the upgrade is going and a green bar along the bottom of the screen gives a rough indication of how far things have progressed (Figure 1.29).

Eventually the final stages of installation will be reached, and the window of Figure 1.30 will appear. It is not mandatory to use your product key in

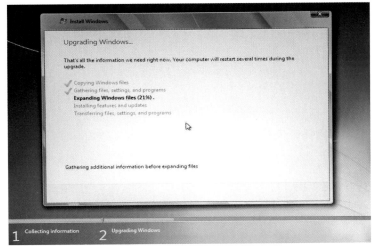

Fig.1.29 *The green bargraph shows how things are progressing*

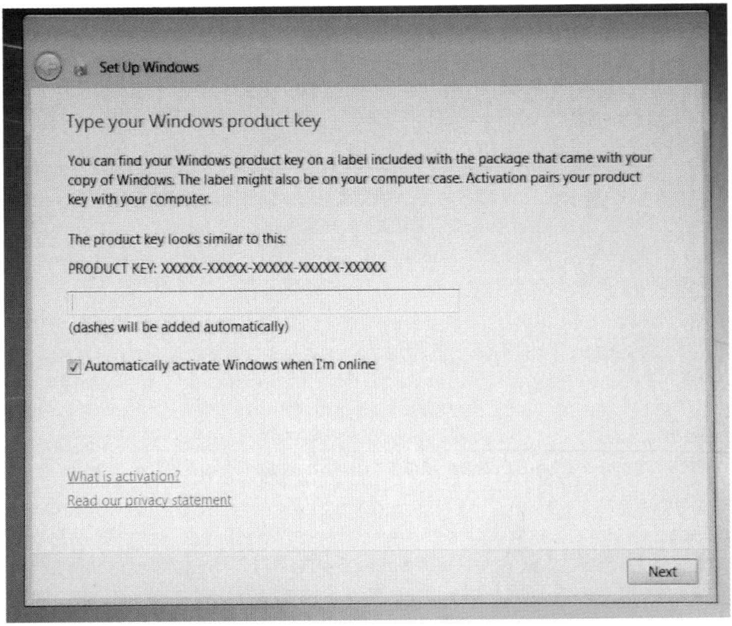

Fig.1.30 *Your product key can be entered here*

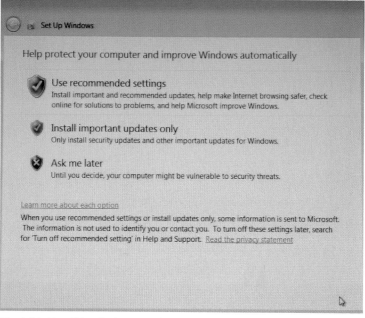

Fig.1.31 Use this window to select the required type of updates

order to upgrade Windows 7, but it is needed in order to activate the program and keep it working beyond the 30-day trial period. Therefore, it is probably best to enter it into the textbox at this stage. Note that it is the product key supplied with the Windows 7 upgrade that is needed here, and not the product key of the Vista installation.

There is the option of automatically activating the program as part of the installation process. Tick the checkbox if you wish to use this method, which is the easiest way of handling product activation. However, it will obviously require the PC to have an active Internet connection. Also, it is probably best to get Windows 7 installed and running to your satisfaction before activating your copy and tying it to a particular PC.

The next window (Figure 1.31) is used to determine the way that automatic updates of Windows will be handled. It is not essential to opt for automatic updates at this stage, since it is possible to switch on automatic any time after the upgrade has been completed. It is also possible to manually download updates once the upgrade has been installed. However, if

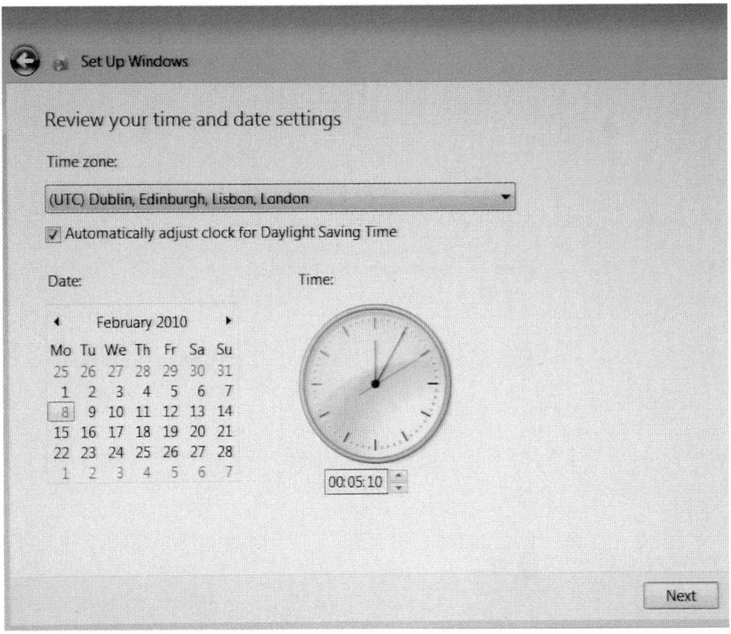

Fig.1.32 The time, date, and time zone should already be correct

you use a broadband connection it is probably best to opt to at least download important updates automatically.

At the next window (Figure 1.32) the time, date, and time zone are set. It should not be necessary to make any changes here, as this information should have been transferred from the Vista installation. The computer used in this example has a wireless Internet connection, and the

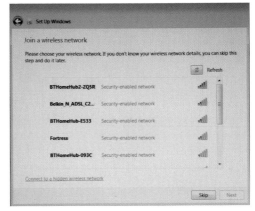

Fig.1.33 The appropriate network is selected

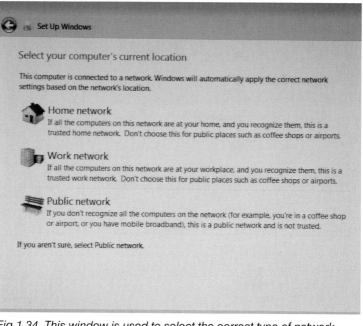

Fig.1.34 This window is used to select the correct type of network

window of Figure 1.33 enables the appropriate wi-fi network to be selected. This window will not appear if any form of wired Internet connection is used. Instead, the Setup program will go straight to the window of Figure 1.34 where the appropriate type of network is selected. Finally, the computer should boot into Windows 7 (Figure 1.35), and the upgrade is complete.

Final touches

The computer should be much as it was when running Vista, but there are some differences between Vista and Windows 7 that will enforce a few changes. Also, there could be a few minor inadequacies in the upgrade process that will make it necessary to fix a few things manually in order to get everything working properly. Having installed the upgrade, expect to put in a certain amount of time and effort in order to get everything operating entirely to your satisfaction.

Fig.1.35 Finally, the computer has been booted into Windows 7. The icons from the original desktop are all present and correct

In this example upgrade the Upgrade Advisor program had suggested that a new driver program would be needed for the wi-fi card. However, as explained previously, the wi-fi card seemed to work as well as ever, complete with a new and improved user interface. Possibly the original driver was actually all right for use with Windows 7, or perhaps the upgrade program installed an updated version. With something like this it is as well to leave well alone, and not install a driver program that might make matters worse rather than better.

Of course, in most cases where the need for an updated driver was indicated, it will indeed be necessary to install the updated software at this stage. Most driver software is not installed using the standard Windows method, so it is important to read the manufacturer's installation instructions. Follow these instructions precisely, because any slight deviation from the recommended installation method is usually sufficient to prevent the driver from being installed properly.

There might be a few problems with application programs, even if they are fully compatible with Windows 7. In an extreme case it might be necessary to uninstall and reinstall the software in order to get it working properly. Reinstallation is not usually necessary though, and the problem can often be solved by entering the product activation code again, or something of this nature. Sometimes the features of a program that

Fig.1.36 This window gives easy access to a range of useful features

have been customised will revert to their default states. The program will be as it was immediately after installation. It is likely that the only way of rectifying this problem will be to redo the customisation from scratch.

Personalize

It should not be necessary to make changes to things like the screen resolution and colour depth, as these settings will usually be transferred from the Vista installation. You may wish to make some changes to the appearance of Windows 7, and perhaps also to the sounds used by the program. The easiest way of doing this is to first go to the Start menu and left-click the Getting Started menu option. This launches the window of Figure 1.36, which gives easy access to a range of features.

In this case it is the Personalize Windows section that is required, and left-clicking this icon produces the window of Figure 1.37. A selection of backgrounds for the Windows desktop is available here. Note that with the exception of the basic Windows 7 design, these are all slide shows that will slowly cycle the desktop through a set of about half a dozen images. This window gives access to other customisation facilities,

*Fig.1.37 Half a dozen alternative desktop designs are provided. These
are all slide shows rather than static displays*

permitting changes to things such as the sounds used by Windows, the
screen saver, and the desktop icons.

Before upgrading Windows XP

As explained previously, upgrading Windows XP is more complicated
and time consuming than upgrading Vista. With Windows XP it is not
possible to upgrade the existing installation into its Windows 7 equivalent,
complete with all your settings and your programs. The only upgrade
method from Windows XP supported by a Windows 7 upgrade disc is to
install a fresh copy of the new operating system, and then manually
reinstall all the application software. Your Windows settings also have to
be transferred manually or set up from scratch.

I suppose it should actually be possible to upgrade Windows XP, complete
with programs and settings, but only as a two-stage process. First it
would be necessary to upgrade the XP installation to Windows Vista
using the appropriate upgrade disc, and to get the new version of
Windows running properly. Then the Vista installation would have to be
upgraded to Windows 7 using the correct upgrade disc. However, this
method might not be much quicker than upgrading to Windows 7 using
a fresh installation, and it would also involve extra cost since two upgrades

would have to be purchased. It could still be the most practical solution if you do not feel confident about using the fresh installation method.

Assuming that the upgrade from XP will be made by installing Windows 7 from scratch, many of the initial stages are the same as before. Some additional steps might be needed though, and decisions have to be made about the way in which the upgrade will be tackled. Some of the information about upgrading from XP gives the impression that the existing contents of the disc will be wiped and that after the upgrade the disc will contain nothing other than Windows 7. This is not actually the case, but installing Windows 7 does have some major consequences.

The existing Windows installation, together with all the folders and files associated with it are stored on the hard disc drive in a folder called Windows.old. Folders such as Program Files and My Documents will be stored here. Programs installed in Windows XP will not be part of the new installation, and have to be installed again. Data files stored in folders such as My Documents and My Pictures should be left unchanged, and will be in subfolders of the Win.old folder. Data and anything else stored on the hard drive in folders you have generated yourself will not be altered by the new installation, and should still be accessible in the usual way.

It is unlikely that any data files will be lost when Windows 7 is installed, but Microsoft still recommends that backup copies should be made of any important data on the hard disc drive. This is simply general advice, and it is advisable to make sure that backup copies of data are made before undertaking any major change to a computer. In fact data should always be backed up fairly frequently so that a failure of the hard disc can only cause little or no loss of data. Anyway, if there are data files that have not been backed-up, copies of them should be made prior to installing Windows 7.

Programs and settings

The main problem when installing Windows from scratch is that the settings of the original installation will not be automatically transferred to the new one. Also, the application programs that worked fine with the original installation will not be recognised by the freshly installed copy of Windows. The programs therefore have to be installed again, and any customisation of the programs has to be redone.

There is actually a facility within Windows for transferring files and settings from one computer to another, and this can also be used to store settings on a disc and then transfer them back to the same computer after a Windows upgrade. In Windows XP this facility (Figure 1.38) is accessed

Fig.1.38 The first window of the Files and Settings Transfer Wizard

by going to the Start menu and selecting All Programs, Accessories, System, and Files and Settings Transfer Wizard.

It is then a matter of going through the various stages in standard wizard fashion until the required settings have been saved to a disc drive. This facility can also be used to save the specified types of data file. In the current context the option of using a link to another computer is not relevant, and the settings must be saved to a suitable disc drive, which usually means some form of external drive connected to a USB port. However, a network drive can be used.

It is only fair to point out that the Files and Settings Transfer Wizard has some significant limitations. Probably the biggest weakness is that it does not transfer the settings for most application programs. Windows itself will operate much as it did on your old PC, but the same might not be true for the word processor, image editor, accounting program, etc.

As one would expect, the popular Microsoft programs such as Word, Access, and Excel are catered for. Some of the very popular programs from other software companies will also have their settings transferred. The Real Player program, for example, will have its settings moved to

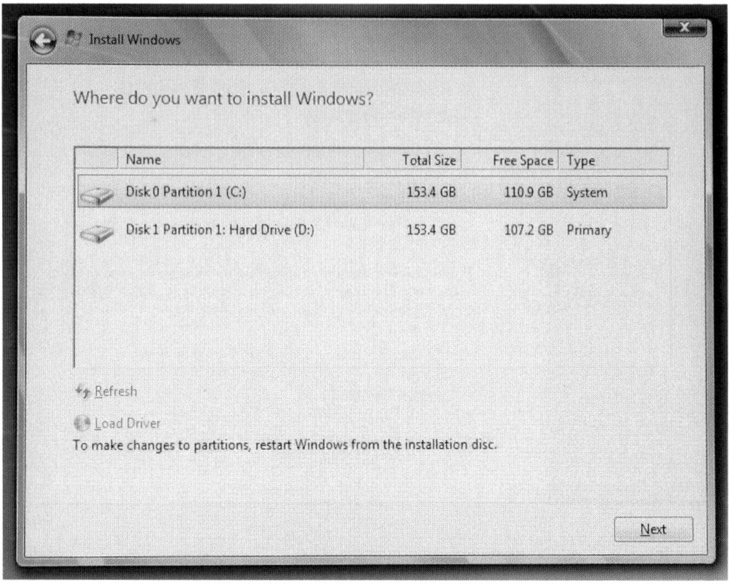

Fig.1.39 Windows is normally installed on drive C:

the new PC. However, few other non-Microsoft applications are supported. Note that it is only the settings for these programs that are transferred, and not the programs themselves. The programs must be installed on the new PC in the usual way before the settings are transferred. Even where the settings for an application program are transferred, any customisation of the program such as changes to toolbars will not necessarily be included.

Windows Easy Transfer

Microsoft offer an alternative way of transferring files and settings in the form of a downloadable program called Windows Easy Transfer. This is a simplified version of the software that is built into Windows XP and Vista, and it will only work with an external USB drive. This is not a major limitation, since this is the transfer method most people will use anyway. This program can be downloaded from the Microsoft web site at this address:

www.windows.microsoft.com/windows-easy-transfer

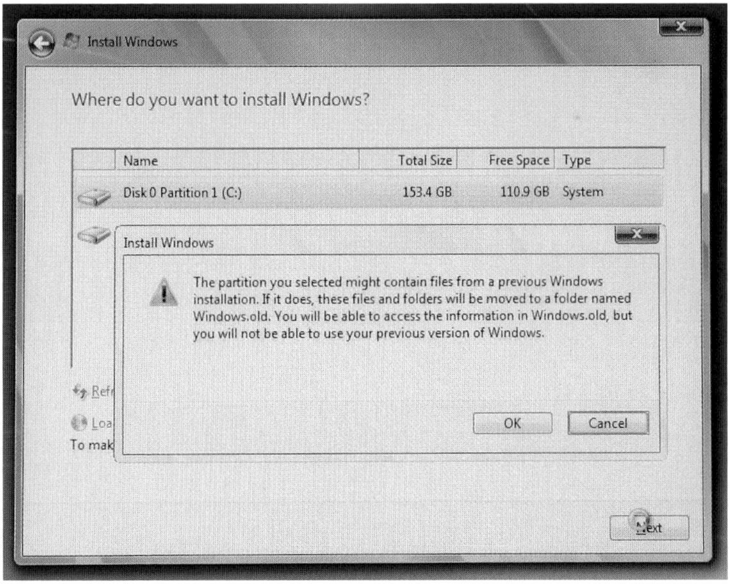

Fig.1.40 Operate the OK button if you are ready to proceed with the upgrade

Note that there are four versions of this program, with 32-bit and 64-bit versions for both XP and Vista. If you decide to use this program, make sure you download the version that matches the operating system running on your PC.

Upgrading from XP

Once the preliminaries are out of the way and you are ready to go ahead with the upgrade, the initial stages are the same as before. However, select the Custom option when the screen of Figure 1.26 is reached. A window similar to the one shown in Figure 1.39 will then appear, but the entries shown here will depend on the hard drives installed, and on their partitioning. In this example there are two hard disc drives, each of them having a single partition. These are drives C: and D: respectively, and it is normally drive C: that is used as the boot drive. This will be selected by default, and it should not be necessary to change this setting.

Operating the Next button should move things on to the warning message of Figure 1.40, which simply explains that any files in an existing Windows

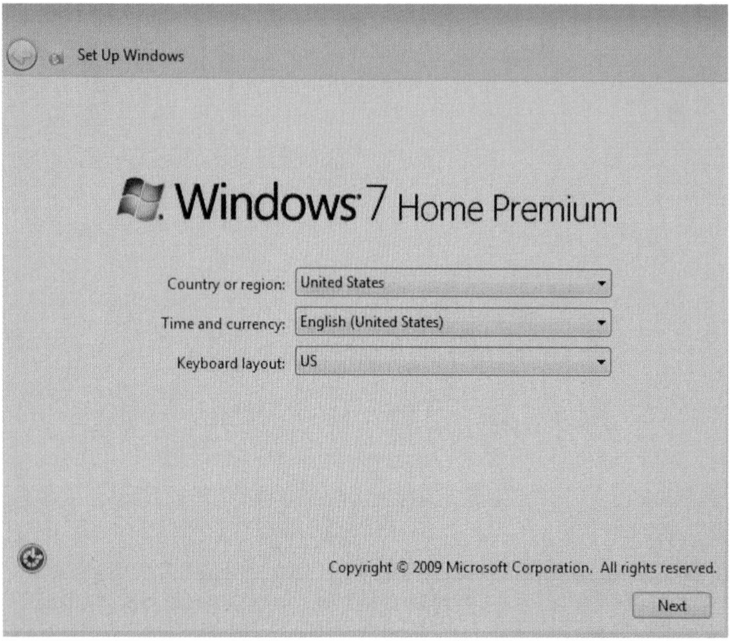

Fig.1.41 Use the drop-down menus to enter the correct country information

installation will be moved into a folder called Windows.old, and that the currently installed programs will no longer be accessible. It is possible that a different message will appear, stating that Windows cannot be installed on the selected partition. Assuming that the selected partition has enough free space for the upgrade, the most likely cause of the problem is that the hard disc drive is formatted using the old FAT32 system. Windows XP can operate using a FAT32 boot drive, or with one that uses the later NTFS disc filing system, but Windows 7 and Vista can only use a NTFS drive. The solution to the problem is to exit the Setup program, run the FAT32 to NTFS conversion utility that is included in Windows XP, and then start the upgrade process again.

The installation process is then much the same as before, but a fresh installation is usually a bit faster than an upgrade. It can still take an hour or more though, with the computer rebooting itself a few times along the way. The final stages involve a few additional steps, because a fresh installation does not extract any information from an existing installation.

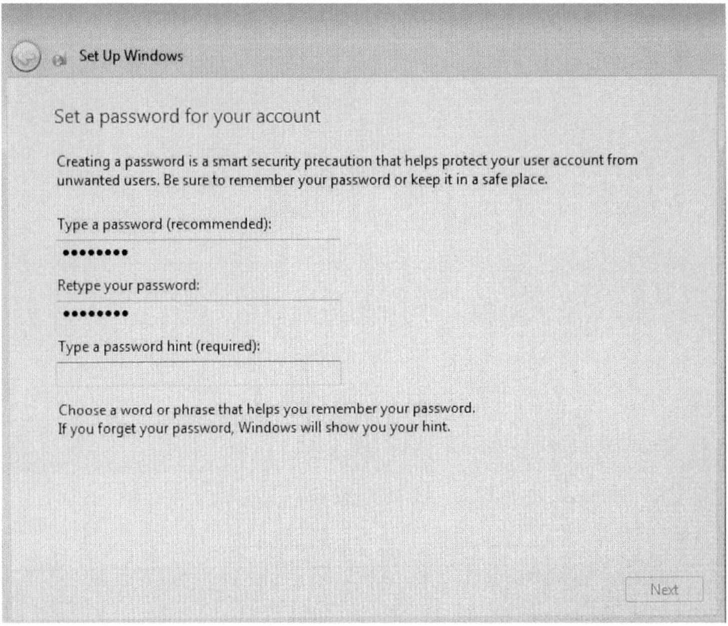

Fig.1.42 If required, the account can be password protected

At the window of Figure 1.41 you have to provide country information via the three drop-down menus.

There will be another window where a name for the computer and an account name are specified. Of course, these do not have to be the same ones that were used with the original Windows XP installation, but it is probably best to use the same names. A further window (Figure 1.42) enables an optional account password to be entered, together with a password hint. Again, it is not essential to adhere to the scheme of things used with the original installation, but life will probably be easier if you keep things familiar and do so.

Eventually you should end up with the computer booted into Windows 7, and a rather blank looking desktop (Figure 1.43). At this stage no settings have been transferred from the original Windows installation, and the only icon on the desktop is the one for the Recycle Bin, which is part of a default Windows installation. Either manually or automatically, the computer must now have the settings added, data files restored, and the application programs installed, but any updating of the drivers

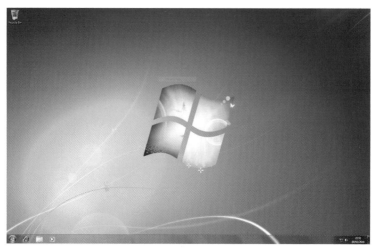

Fig.1.43 The computer has successfully booted into Windows 7

or other finishing touches to the Windows installation should be completed first.

It might be necessary to alter the screen resolution, and this can be done by going to the Windows Control Panel (Figure 1.13) and operating the "Adjust screen resolution" link in the Appearance and Personalization section. There is a drop-down slider control in the new window that appears (Figure 1.44), and this is used to set the required resolution. When you operate the Apply button Windows will ask whether you wish to confirm the change or revert to the original setting. This is really included as a sort of safety measure. If the monitor cannot handle the selected resolution and an unusable display is produced, it will not be possible to confirm the change because the dialogue box will not be visible. After several seconds the screen resolution will be returned automatically to its previous setting, and a usable display should return.

The Control Panel offers other facilities that might be needed in order to get the computer fully working in the required fashion. If the original Windows installation was set up with more than one account, it will be necessary to add one or more user accounts, since only one is provided during installation. There is a facility for adding or removing accounts in the User Accounts and Family Safety section.

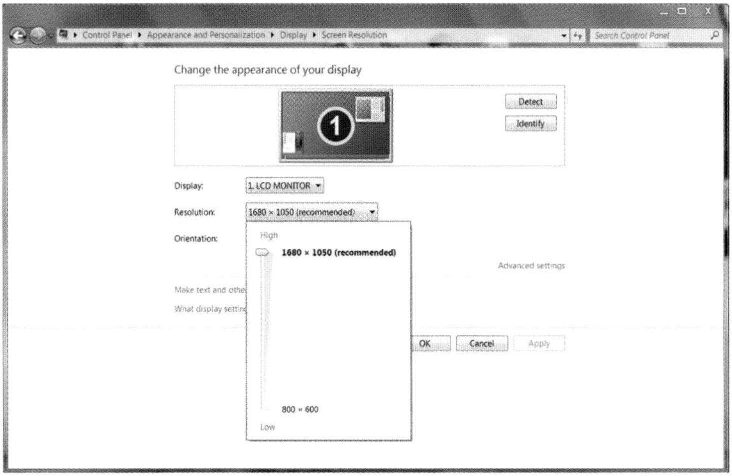

Fig.1.44 Use the slider control to set the required screen resolution

Fig.1.45 The initial screen of the Windows Easy Transfer utility

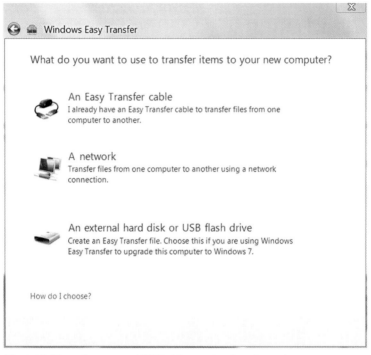

Fig.1.46 Here the external USB drive option is selected

Easy transfer

The Windows Easy Transfer program is used when transferring files and settings, but it does not have to be downloaded from the Microsoft site. It is part of a standard Windows 7 installation, and it is launched by going to the Getting Started section of the Control Panel (Figure 1.36) and activating the "Transfer files and settings from another computer" link. This produces the initial window of Figure 1.45 that is really just an information screen, and then the window of Figure 1.46 where the external USB drive option is selected. It is then just a matter of going through the remaining steps, which are handled in standard wizard fashion.

2

Prevention

Safety first

Modern versions of Windows are less prone to problems than some of the early varieties, and one reason for this is the improved security of Vista and Windows 7. These operating systems are sometimes criticised for making it difficult for users to change some files, or even to find them at all on the hard disc drive, but these security measures reduce the risk of inexperienced users accidentally damaging the operating system. The downside is that making changes to the system can be a trifle more difficult for experienced users.

A modern version of Windows such as Windows 7 also tends to be better at extricating itself from errors and problems, and in many cases it will recover without the need for any assistance from the user. With some versions of Windows there could be major problems if the power failed while the computer was running, or if someone switched off the computer instead of shutting down Windows in the correct manner. This type of thing is unlikely to faze Windows 7, but it is still better to do things in the correct manner and avoid the possibility of producing unnecessary problems. It is definitely a case of "prevention is better than cure".

Keeping up-to-date

Security from outside attack is another aspect of Windows that has been significantly improved over the years. Even so, security "holes" are found in Windows fairly regularly, and software patches to seal them are issued by Microsoft. Particularly with a computer that has an Internet connection, it is important that these patches are downloaded and installed as soon as possible. As pointed out in Chapter 1, it is a good idea to opt for automatic updates during the upgrade process. It is only necessary to take the option for important updates in order to receive security patches.

In order to check the current status of the Windows Automatic Updates feature, or to make changes to the settings, launch the Control Panel from the Start menu and the use the drop-down menu near the top right-

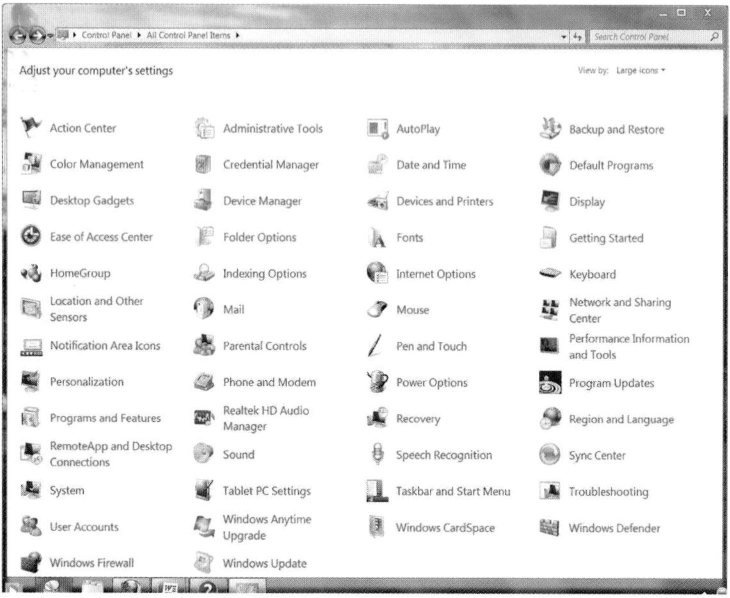

Fig.2.1 The Control Panel set to the Large Icon view

hand corner of the window to select one of the icon views. In the new version of the Control Panel (Figure 2.1) there will be a Windows Update link near the bottom of the window, and activating this link changes the window to one that shows the current settings and state of this facility (Figure 2.2).

If you wish to change something, operate the Change Setting link in the right-hand section of the window. The window should then look something like Figure 2.3, but the exact appearance will obviously depend on

Fig.2.2 The Windows Update window

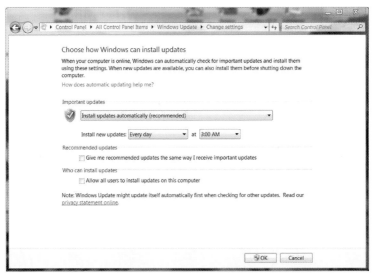

Fig.2.3 Use this window to select the required type of updating

the current settings used for your computer. The large drop-down menu is used to choose from fully automatic updates, semi-automatic updates, manual updates, or none at all. With semi-automatic operation you select the automatically downloaded updates that should be installed.

With manual operation nothing is downloaded automatically, and you are prompted to select the required downloads from a list. Using manual selection is probably best if an ordinary dial-up connection is used, or you have a capped broadband link with a monthly allowance that is not very generous. Pointless downloads can be avoided by only selecting downloads that are important or of real benefit to you. Note that the actual size of downloads varies enormously. Some are well under a megabyte, whereas something like a Windows service pack can be several hundred megabytes. While some of the larger downloads may be very desirable, they are probably not a practical proposition unless some form of broadband Internet connection is available. A large download such as a major service pack is usually made available on disc as well.

If you opt for automatic updates, but with only the important ones being included, it is still possible to download and install updates manually. This method can also be used if automatic updating is switched off

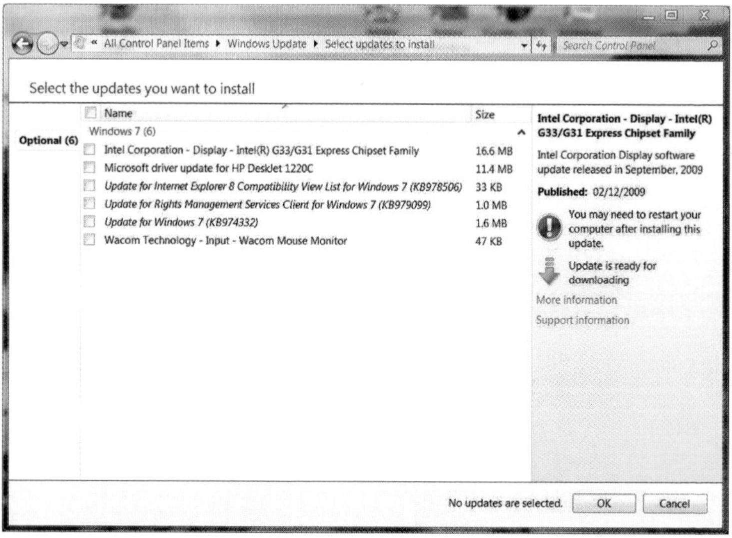

Fig.2.4 This window lists the available updates

completely. From the window of Figure 2.2, operate the "Check for updates" link. If any updates are available they will be listed, as in Figure 2.4. Tick the checkboxes for any updates that you wish to install, and then operate the OK button. The window will then change to one like Figure 2.5, showing the number of downloads selected and their total size.

Fig.2.5 This window shows the selected updates and their total size

Operate the Back button in the top left-hand corner of the window if you wish to make changes or left-click the Install Updates button to go ahead with the updating process. If you decide to proceed, you will be kept informed of progress (Figure 2.6). It is possible to carry on computing while

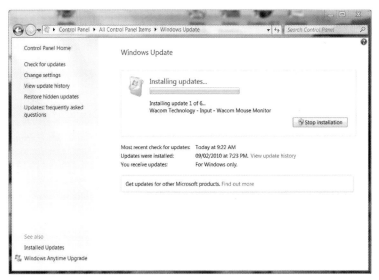

Fig.2.6 You are kept informed about how the updates are progressing

the updates are installed, but it is probably best to close all application programs prior to updating the computer. Updates often require the computer to be rebooted, and several reboots might be needed if a number of downloads are being installed. Any applications that are running have to be shut down before the computer can be rebooted.

Do not tweak

Probably the only sure-fire way of preventing Windows from getting into difficulties is to never install any applications programs at all, which is not exactly a practical proposition. However, you can certainly reduce the risk of problems occurring by following some simple rules. Experienced users fiddle around with the Windows configuration files and manage to customise the user interface in ways that are not normally possible. This is fine for those having suitable experience of Windows, because they know what they are doing. They can largely avoid problems and can soon backtrack to safety if something should go wrong.

Inexperienced users are almost certain to damage the operating system if they try this sort of tweaking, and will not have the expertise to quickly sort things out when problems arise. Just the opposite in fact, and one thing can lead to another, with the operating system soon getting beyond redemption. If you are not an expert on the inner workings of Windows it is best not to delve into its configuration files. A great deal of customisation can be done using the normal Windows facilities, and there are applications programs that enable further customisation to be undertaken without having to directly alter files.

Even if you are familiar with previous versions of Windows and their inner workings, it is not a good idea to start hacking into Windows 7 as if it was an earlier version of Windows. Although there are superficial similarities between the various versions of Windows, there are also major differences in their inner workings. Things that are acceptable with Windows ME might not have the desired effect with Windows 7, if they are permissible at all. Although Windows 7 and Vista have much in common, it is still by no means certain that a tweak for one will have the desired effect with the other. If you really must tinker with Windows 7, gain some experience with this operating system and learn as much about it as possible before you start altering things.

Careful deletion

In the days of MS/DOS it was perfectly acceptable to delete a program and any files associated with it if you no longer wished to use the program. Matters are very different with any version of Windows from Windows 95 onwards, where most software is installed into the operating system. There are actually some simple programs that have just one file, and which do not require any installation, but these are few and far between these days.

Most programs are installed onto the computer using an installation program, and this program does not simply make folders on the hard disc and copy files into them from the CD-ROM. It will also make changes to the Windows configuration files so that the program is properly integrated with the operating system. In particular, it will make changes to the Windows Registry. If you simply delete the program's directory structure to get rid of it, Windows will not be aware that the program has been removed. During the boot-up process the operating system will probably look for files associated with the deleted program, and will produce error messages when it fails to find them.

There is another potential problem in that Windows utilises shared files. This is where one file, such as a DLL type, is shared by two or more programs. In deleting a program and the other files in its directory structure you could also be deleting files needed by other programs. This could prevent other programs from working properly, or even from starting up at all. If a program is loaded onto the hard disc using an installation program, the only safe way of removing it is to use either the uninstaller program supplied with the program, or the standard Windows uninstaller facility. Uninstalling programs was covered in chapter one and will not be considered further here.

Beta problems

Both old and brand new software are potential sources of problems with Windows. Old programs can be problematic because they do not adhere to the current rules for Windows software. In the case of brand new software it is the Beta test versions or any other versions prior to the commercial release that are the main problem. These are not fully tried and tested, and cannot be guaranteed to do things "by the book".

In all probability, some sections of the code will contain programming errors and simply will not work properly. People who make a living testing this type of software almost invariably use one PC for testing the software and a second PC for other purposes. That way there is no major loss if the test software runs amok and deletes half the files on the hard disc! If you do not have a second PC for use with dubious software it is best not to try it at all.

At one time the initial commercial releases of programs were not always reliable, and some software publishers seemed to be guilty of getting their customers to unwittingly do the final testing for them. This sort of thing may still go on in some niche markets, but it is thankfully something of a rarity these days. The cost of sending out replacement discs plus the loss of reputation makes it an unsustainable tactic. These days, new software whether it is totally new or an upgrade version, should be very reliable. In the past it was advisable to let new software mature before buying it, but this should no longer be necessary.

New software might contain a few minor bugs, but there should be nothing that will seriously damage your Windows installation. If new software should prove troublesome, there should be a help-line that can give advice on the problem. Software publishers' web sites often have software patches that can fix any obscure problems that have come to light after the final versions of the programs have been sent out to the shops.

Memory

In the early days of Windows 95 it was not unusual for things to grind to a halt, usually with the dreaded red exclamation mark appearing on the screen, complete with a brief error message. In fact, there seemed to be one or two of these messages every time someone used a PC. Thankfully, this type of thing is relatively rare these days. There were probably two main reasons for these early problems, and one of them was a lack of memory in the PCs of the day. At that time memory was quite expensive. Eight megabytes of RAM was quite typical, and 16 megabytes was considered to be a large amount of memory. Software manufacturers were eager for their programs to appeal to as many people as possible, which often led them to be overoptimistic about the system requirements. If the requirements listed 8 megabytes of memory as the minimum and recommended at least 16 megabytes should be used, then 16 megabytes was probably the minimum that would really give trouble free and usable results.

These days memory is relatively cheap, and PCs are mostly well endowed in this respect. On the other hand, programs, including operating systems, seem to require ever more memory. Also, many users now have two or more programs running simultaneously, probably with several background tasks running as well. If you run memory hungry programs on a computer that has a modest amount of memory and error messages keep on appearing, it is worth investing in some extra memory. Even if it does not cure the problem, Windows and your programs will almost certainly run more quickly. If you wish to run a couple of major applications under Windows 7 there is a lot to be said for having at least two gigabytes of RAM installed in your PC. With memory costing relatively little these days, many users now opt for three gigabytes, which is the maximum for most PCs when running a 32-bit version of Windows.

Defragmenters

Many users tend to assume that files are automatically stored on the hard disc on the basis of one continuous section of disc per file. Unfortunately, it does not necessarily operate in this fashion. When Windows is first installed on a PC it is likely that files will be added in this fashion. The applications programs are then installed, and things will probably continue in an organised fashion with files stored on the disc as single clumps of data. Even if things have progressed well thus far, matters soon take a turn for the worse when the user starts deleting files, adding new files or programs, deleting more files, and so on.

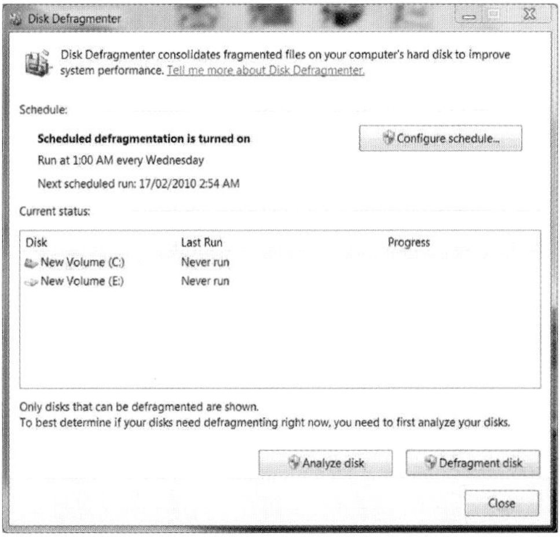

Gaps are produced in the continuous block of data when files are deleted. Windows utilises the gaps when new data is added, but it will use them even if each one is not large enough to take a complete file. If necessary, it will use dozens of these small vacant areas to accommodate a large file. This can result in a large file being spread across the disc in numerous tiny packets of data,

Fig.2.7 The drives that can be processed are listed here

which makes reading the file a relatively slow and inefficient business. The computer can seriously slow down when a substantial number of files get fragmented in this way.

There are programs called defragmenters that reorganise the files on a disc drive so that, as far as reasonably possible, large files are not fragmented. A program of this type is available in the System Tools submenu as the Disk Defragmenter (Start – Accessories – System Tools – Disk Defragmenter). This utility has something of a chequered past, and in older versions of Windows it gave odd results with some disc drives. At some point in the proceedings the estimated time to completion would start to rise and usually kept rising with the process never finishing! Provided you are using a reasonably modern version of Windows there should be no problem of this type and the Disk Defragmenter program should work well. There should certainly be no problem with the Windows 7 version.

On launching the defragmenter program a window like the one shown in Figure 2.7 is produced. The main panel lists the disc drives that can be processed by the program, and in this case the computer's two hard disc drives are listed. These are physically two separate hard disc drives, but it is actually the logical disc drives that the program lists. In other words, if the computer has (say) one hard disc drive with three partitions, each partition will be listed separately. The partitions are treated as three

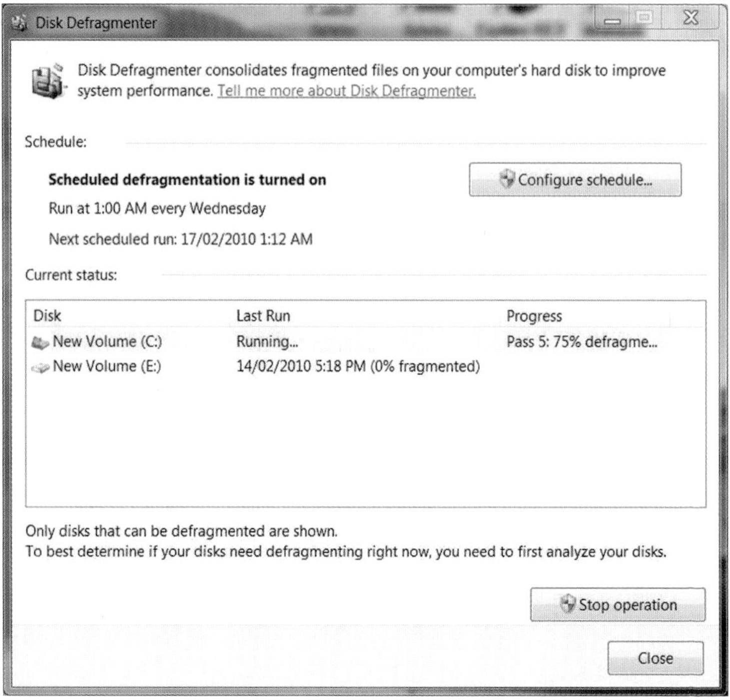

Fig.2.8 The program gives details of how things are progressing

separate entities by the operating system, and they are therefore processed in that way by defragmenter programs.

While it is possible to jump straight in and start processing the selected drive, this version of Disk Defragmenter offers the alternative of first analysing the drive to determine how badly (or otherwise) it is fragmented. There is little point in wasting time defragmenting a disc that is performing well. To analyse the disc operate the Analyze Disk button near the bottom of the window. The test result is in the form of a percentage, and Microsoft recommends defragmenting the disc if the result is ten percent or more.

In this case drive C: did require defragmentation, but with a result of zero percent for drive D:, it was only drive C: that needed processing. Drive C: was therefore selected and the Defragment Disk button was operated. The program keeps you informed of what it is doing Figure 2.8, but unlike most previous versions it does not give an estimate of the remaining time required to complete the task. It is not usually quick though, and can take an hour or more with a large disc that is badly fragmented. It is always not possible to fully defragment the disc, and it is not really necessary to do so. The program should defragment the disc enough to give a significant improvement in performance, and to get the drive operating at something close to its optimum level.

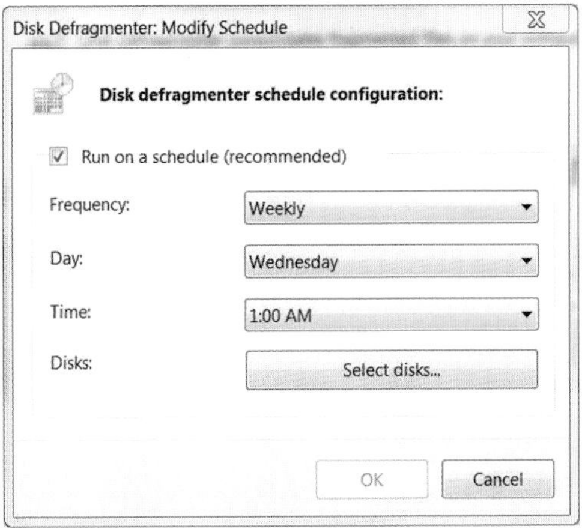

Disk Defragmenter: Modify Schedule

Disk defragmenter schedule configuration:

☑ Run on a schedule (recommended)

Frequency: Weekly ▼

Day: Wednesday ▼

Time: 1:00 AM ▼

Disks: Select disks...

OK | Cancel

Fig.2.9 Use the drop-down menus to set the required schedule

Regular use of Disk Defragmenter should get the disc to the point where it is fully defragmented, or nearly so, and should maintain it close to optimum performance. The defragmenter program can be set to run automatically, and the idea is to schedule it to run at a time when the computer will usually be operating, but will be receiving little or no use. In order to schedule automatic operation it is merely necessary to operate the Configure Schedule button, and then use the dialogue box (Figure 2.9) the select the required time and frequency, and the disc or discs to be processed.

Keeping fit

There are commercial programs available that help to keep PCs running efficiently and reduce the risk of them grinding to a halt. TuneUp Utilities (Figure 2.10) is one of the most popular of these programs, and in common with most software of this type, many of its facilities are designed to optimise performance rather than to keep everything running smoothly. However, its Maintenance section can be used to schedule regular scans (Figure 2.11) that look for errors in the Windows installation, and in most cases the errors will also be corrected.

What does a tune-up program actually do? To some extent a program of this type simply performs general tasks of the type described in this chapter, and most of them at least partially duplicate the built-in system

Fig.2.10 The main window of TuneUp Utilities 2010

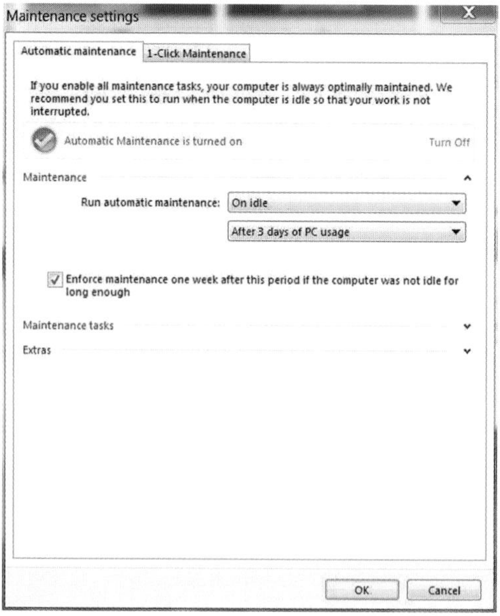

Fig.2.11 Regular scanning can be set up

maintenance tools of Windows. However, most will provide additional features, such as a facility that checks the Windows Registry and tries to correct any errors that are found. Perhaps the main attraction of these programs is that most of them will perform a wide range of tasks automatically, or by running just one program. This makes them very quick and convenient to use.

There are plenty of tuning utilities available for computers that use

Windows, but you need to be careful when using any software of this type. Firstly, make sure that it is intended for use with the version of Windows that you are running. Using a tune-up utility designed for use with something other than the version of Windows you are actually using could result in the operating system being seriously damaged instead of streamlined. I had to replace TuneUp Utilities 2009 with TuneUp Utilities 2010 when upgrading to Windows 7.

Also make sure that the program you are intending to use is from a reputable software company. Unfortunately, some unscrupulous companies have used software of this type as a means of installing various pieces of adware, etc., onto users' computers. Reading reviews of various programs on the Internet and in the computer press should help you to avoid programs that are not what they seem, or simply do not work very well.

Malware

All too often these days the cause of a computer running very slowly or refusing to run at all is not due to a hardware fault or the operating system becoming accidentally damaged, but is instead due to some form of malware. In other words, the computer has become infected with some form of malicious software. There are numerous types of malware currently in circulation, and they attack the computer in various ways. Some malicious programs run unseen in the background, using the computer's resources, and causing it to slow down. Other malicious programs attack the operating system, possibly damaging it to the point where the computer will no longer boot into Windows.

This is definitely something where "prevention is better than cure". Many types of malicious software can be removed successfully without causing any damage to the operating system and the files on the hard disc drive, but others will rapidly cause large amounts of damage to the system as soon as they become established. By the time you realise that there is something amiss it is too late to prevent the damage, and you can reasonably expect to spend a great deal of time sorting things out.

It is important to realise that things have moved on from what might be termed the traditional computer virus. An ordinary virus attaches itself to other files and tries to propagate itself across the system and on to other systems if the opportunity arises. At some stage the virus will make its presence obvious by placing a message on the screen and (or) starting to damage files. Not all viruses try to do any real damage, but a substantial percentage of them will do so unless they are removed first.

Computer security has become more important with the rise in use of the Internet and Email. The original viruses were designed to spread themselves across any system whenever the opportunity arose. In most cases the purpose was to damage the file system of any infected computer. Many of the recent pests are more sinister than this, and in many cases will not actually try to cause significant damage to the file system. Instead, they aid hackers to hijack your PC, extract information from it such as passwords, or something of this nature. If a computer pest is causing your PC to run slowly this could be the least of your problems! Some form of protection from malware is essential for anyone using the Internet.

Likely candidates

A good starting point if you suspect that there could be an "intruder" present in your PC is to investigate the running applications and processes using the Windows Task Manager. With Windows 7 the Task Manager can be launched using the Control – Shift – Escape key combination. Once Task Manager is running you can look for any programs or processes that should not be there. If you are not sure about any of them it is easy to find details using a search engine such as Google. Use the name of the process plus the word "process" as the search string, and several links to sites giving basic details of it.

A program called Hijackthis is a available as a free download from the usual sources such as download.com, and this can be used to show a list of changes to the system and suspicious processes. However, be aware that most of the things it lists will be perfectly legitimate processes and changes. In order to use a program such as this you need a fair amount of expertise, or must obtain specialist help from one of the web sites that offer assistance in dealing with computer infections.

Having found a malicious program by whatever means, you can use the normal search facilities of Windows Explorer to locate and delete the offending program file. Do not be surprised if the offending program simply reappears the next time the computer is booted into Windows. Many modern computer pests are designed so that a file is installed and run each time the computer is booted into the operating system. Hence the deleted program runs again when the computer is rebooted.

In order to permanently remove most modern computer infections it is necessary to use an antivirus program. New PCs are almost invariably supplied complete with a commercial antivirus program, but this usually has a fairly short subscription to updates. After a month or three the virus database is no longer updated with details of new viruses, and the program then becomes less and less effective with the passage of time.

Built-in protection

There are better ways of handling things than continuing to use a commercial antivirus program that is relying on out of date virus definitions. Windows 7 does actually have a built-in program called Windows Defender that is primarily designed to protect the computer from spyware. Software of this type gathers information from your computer and then sends it to a third party. Sometimes this information is fairly innocuous and merely concerns your surfing habits, but spyware can be more sinister in nature.

Windows Defender is normally included as part of a standard Windows 7 installation, so it will almost certainly run automatically each time your computer is switched on. However, it is important to realise that Windows Defender is not a complete solution to keeping malware at bay, and it was never designed to be. It needs to be used in conjunction with an antivirus program.

Note that antivirus software is often in the form of a suite of programs that includes an antispyware program. It is not a good idea to have two programs of this type working simultaneously, so Windows Defender is usually switched off if an alternative program is installed as part of a suite of antivirus software. Also note that if you do use Windows Defender it is important that the Windows Automatic Updates feature is used to at least download and install important updates. This ensures that the Windows Defender database remains up to date and that the program functions effectively.

Real-time protection

Windows Defender runs in the background, protecting your computer all the time it is switched on, which is generally known as "real-time" protection. This is the way that most antivirus software operates, and this is probably the only type that is worth using. Real-time antivirus software tries primarily to prevent malware from getting into the computer in the first place, rather than letting it enter the system and dealing with it later. The flaw in this second approach is that a great deal of harm can be done before the malware is detected and removed.

Fig.2.12 The homepage for the AVG Free program

Sometimes malware is not detected when it is downloaded onto the computer, but it does trigger the antivirus software when it is run and it attempts to alter the system, install further malware, or whatever. This is another aspect of real-time protection, and an important one. It gives a second line of defence that can still prevent the malware from doing any harm.

Free protection

If you do not wish to pay for a subscription to commercial antivirus software there are some good free alternatives available. One option is to use a free online virus checking facility to periodically scan your PC, but the drawback of this method is that there is no real-time protection for your PC. By the time you do a virus scan it is possible that a virus could have been spreading across your files for some time. By the time it is detected and removed it is likely that a significant amount of damage would already have been done.

The alternative to using online virus scanning is to download and install a free antivirus program. There are a few totally free antivirus programs available on the Internet, where you do not even have to pay for any online updates to the database. The free version of AVG 9.0 from Grisoft is one that is certainly worth trying, as is the free version of Avast Antivirus 5.0. Here we will concentrate on the free version of AVG 9.0. The Grisoft site is at:

www.grisoft.com

On the home page there might be a link to the free version of the program, but it does not seem to feature quite as prominently in the home page as it did in the past. At the time of writing this, the web address for Grisoft's free software is (Figure 2.12):

http://free.avg.com/download-avg-anti-virus-free-edition

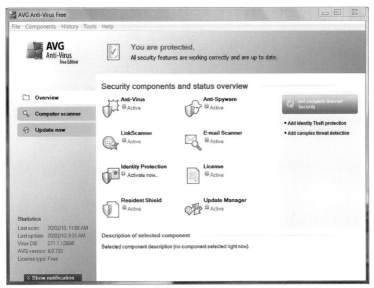

Fig.2.13 The Overview section of AVG Free 9.0

There is an instruction manual for the program in PDF format, and it is possible to read this online provided your PC has the Adobe Acrobat Reader program installed. However, it is definitely a good idea to download the manual and store it on the hard disc drive so that it is handy for future reference. It is a good idea to at least take a quick look through the manual which, amongst other things, provides installation instructions. However, installation is fairly straightforward and follows along the normal lines for Windows software.

Daily updates to AVG are available free of charge, so although free, it should always be reasonably up-to-date provided the updates are regularly downloaded and installed. This program has a reputation for being very efficient, and it did once detect a couple of backdoor Trojan programs on my system that a certain well known commercial program had failed to detect. It is certainly one of the best freebies on the Internet, and it generally performs very well in comparison to commercial equivalents.

AVG has a useful range of facilities and it is a very capable program. Like Windows Defender, it runs in the background and provides real-time protection, but you can also go into the main program. It can be launched via the normal routes, and by default there will be a quick-

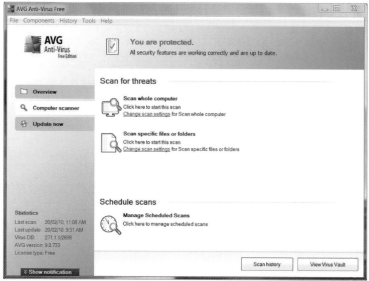

Fig.2.14 The whole computer or selected files and folders can be scanned

launch button near the bottom left-hand corner of the Windows Desktop. The program has various sections, and the initial window provides access to them (Figure 2.13). There is a facility here that manually updates the program's virus database, but the program will automatically update provided an active Internet link is available when the program is booted into Windows.

In common with most antivirus programs you can set it to scan the system on a regular basis. It is also possible to manually start a scan, and you then have the option of either scanning the entire computer, or just scanning some selected files or folders (Figure 2.14). If you think that a downloaded file is a bit suspect, it is therefore possible to scan that particular file without having to scan every other file on the computer as well.

When a scan of the computer is completed you are provided with a summary of the results (Figure 2.15). In this example the AVG program has found three infections that are actually in a single archive file. These are unhealed infections, which in the terminology of antivirus programs means that the program cannot remove the infections without damaging the file or files in which the infections are located. Bear in mind here, that computer infections are often in the form of software that is buried

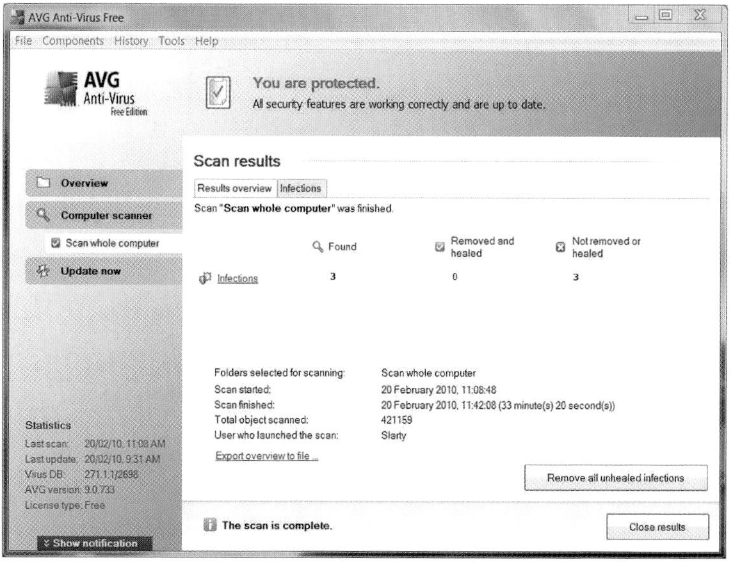

Fig.2.15 The scan has found three infections

somewhere in larger files. In order to get rid of the infections it can be necessary to remove the files that contain them. In order to get AVG to remove the infections it is just a matter of operate the "Remove all unhealed infections" button.

Rather than being deleted, some files are moved to what in AVG terminology is called the "virus vault". The idea of a virus vault is to render the infection harmless by keeping it on the hard disc in a fashion that prevents it from being activated. It can be reinstated if a mistake has been made and it turns out that the infection is actually an important file that is harmless. This is unlikely, but so-called "false positives" can occur, and the virus vault method makes it easy to restore a file if a mistake should occur. Files in the virus vault can be deleted once you are sure that they are genuine infections and that they are not needed.

Extras

The free version of AVG 9.0 lacks all the features of the full program, but it is nevertheless much more than a basic antivirus program. As already pointed out, there are various sections that can be accessed from the initial window (Figure 2.13). In addition to the antivirus feature there is

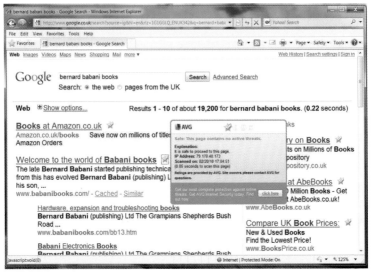

Fig.2.16 Web pages are checked before they are viewed

an anti-spyware program, and with the AVG program installed this takes over from Windows Defender, which is switched off.

There is also an Email scanner and a link scanner. The latter tries to prevent the computer from becoming infected from an attack site when surfing the web. When using the Google search engine for example, it places a green tick against search results where a scan has shown the pages to be a safe (Figure 2.16), or a warning is given if a link leads to a suspect page. This feature works in conjunction with the Firefox and Internet Explorer web browsers and with certain search engines. It does increase the loading on the microprocessor and slows things down a little when surfing the net, but it greatly reduces the risk when visiting sites of unknown authenticity.

Awkward infections

It is only fair to point out that an antivirus program can not automatically remove every type of computer infection. Most can be dealt with automatically, but some of the more awkward ones have to be removed manually. In such cases the program will usually provide removal instructions, or take you to a web site where detailed instructions can be found.

Some of the steps required can be a bit technical, and in some cases it is necessary to manually edit the Windows Registry. Everything should be fine provided you follow the instructions "to the letter". However, if you have a friend or relative who has a fair amount of computing expertise, enlisting their help is probably a good idea, for peace of mind if nothing else.

Second opinion

As explained previously, online virus scanning sites are not really suitable as the main way of keeping malware at bay, because they do not provide real-time protection. On the other hand, they are invaluable if you suspect that your PC has an infection but your antivirus program is failing to detect anything amiss. Modern antivirus programs are very good at detecting and dealing with a wide range of computer infections, but no program of this type is perfect.

In cases where you have good reason to suspect that all is not well, but your normal antivirus software fails to bring anything to light, it is worthwhile getting a second opinion from an online virus scanner. In fact it could be worth trying a couple of them. If three different scans fail to find anything, it is likely that the problem has its cause elsewhere, and it is time to start exploring other avenues.

Note that some of the online virus scanners are basically just that, and will do no more than report any threats that are found. If an infection is detected you will probably be given the name of the infected file, the name of the infection, and any other important information. The scanner will not try to remove the problem, and it is left to you to sort things out. Other online scanners are more helpful and will, as far as possible, deal with any

Fig.2.17 The BitDefender online scanner

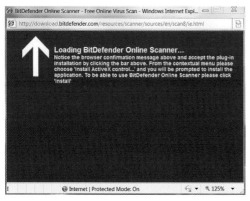

Fig.2.18 Download instructions are provided

infections that are found. It is probably best to use the ones that will try to deal with any problems, and this is especially so if you have limited experience with computers.

As pointed out previously, it is not a good idea to have two security programs of the same type running at the same time.

On the face of it, this means that the existing antivirus software must be deactivated before using an online virus scanner. In most cases this

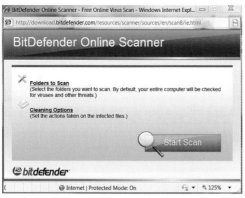

Fig.2.19 Select the areas to be scanned

does not seem to be necessary though. The vast majority of these scanners will work perfectly well and will not cause any problems if the computer has a real-time antivirus program running as well. However, it would be best to check this point before running an online scan. Of course, it is not a good idea to install

another ordinary antivirus program unless the existing one is uninstalled first.

A very useful online virus scan is available from the BitDefender site at this web address (Figure 2.17):

http://www.bitdefender.com/scanner/online/free.html

When the Start Scan button is operated you first have to agree to the licence conditions, and then the window of Figure 2.18 appears. This gives instructions for downloading and installing the scanner. Although these facilities are called online scanners, they seem to invariably involve downloading a program, applet,

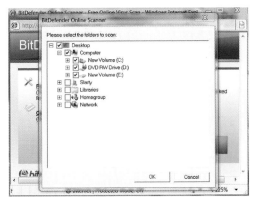

Fig.2.20 Select the drives to be scanned

ActiveX control, or something of this general type, and they are perhaps browser based rather than true online facilities.

The next window (Figure 2.19) enables the user to select the parts of the computer that will be scanned. In the current context it will presumably be the entire computer that is scanned, which is the default setting, but it is possible to select (say) just the drives if desired (Figure 2.20). It is also possible to select the required scan options (Figure 2.21). For example, when a threat is found it can be treated, deleted, or left untouched and reported.

There is an option for using heuristic detection, and this is a feature of many antivirus programs. Antivirus software normally operates by checking the files on your computer against a database of known viruses, Trojans, worms, or whatever. An infection is reported when a file matches one of the malware

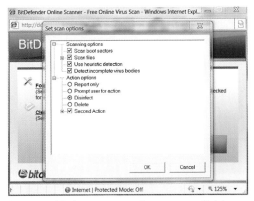

Fig.2.21 Various scan options are available

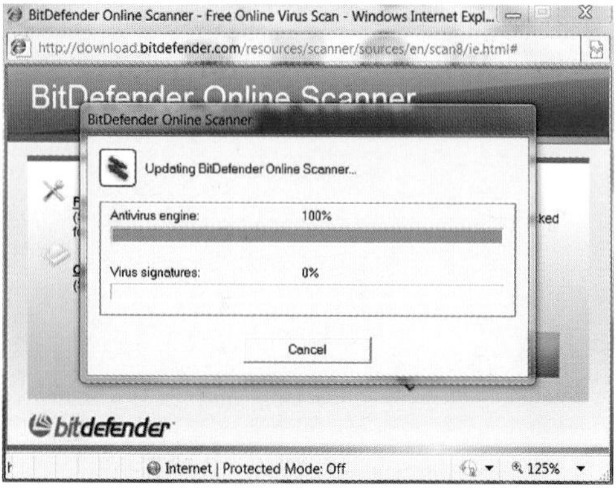

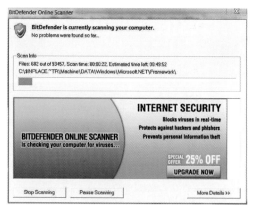

definitions in the database. One problem with this system is that there is inevitably a delay between an infection being let loose on the world and its inclusion in virus databases.

Fig.2.22 The virus database is downloaded

Another problem is that malware writers make frequent but often quite minor changes to their programs so that they quickly cease to match any current virus a database entries. Of course, the new versions are soon discovered and suitable entries are added to the virus databases, but this takes time. The malware producers tend to stay one step ahead of software companies that produce antivirus products.

Heuristic detection is intended to find viruses even if there is no exact match in the virus database. It does this by using more loosely defined rules. For instance, a partial match with an existing virus could be sufficient to trigger a report, instead of requiring an exact match. The heuristic approach increases the chances of finding newly released threats, but it also increases the chances of a threat being reported erroneously. Even so, it is a technique that is widely used in antivirus software, and it is probably best to use this option when it is available.

Fig.2.23 The scan is under way

Operate the Start Scan button when any required changes have been made to the program's settings. There will then be a delay while the virus database is downloaded (Figure 2.22), after which the scan will start (Figure 2.23). There is the usual bargraph to indicate how far the scan has progressed, and there is also an estimate of the

Fig.2.24 No infections were discovered

remaining time until completion. As with anything of this type, it can take a couple of hours of more to scan a system that has a large hard disc drive containing more than a hundred thousand files. Eventually the test results will be provided, and in this example (Figure 2.24) no infections were found.

Firewall

Some computer users tend to confuse firewalls with antivirus software, and think that they are they are different terms for the same thing. This is definitely not the case, and the built-in firewall of Windows 7 should not be regarded as an alternative to anti-virus software. The two types of software are designed to protect computers from outside attack, but they approach the problems in very different ways.

Fig.2.25 The Firewall is switched on

The purpose of a firewall is to stop hackers from gaining access to the files on your PC via a network connection, which in practice usually means via the Internet. A firewall does not provide protection against viruses by trying to detect and disable them. Its function is to block anyone trying to hack into the computer with the intention of introducing malware or stealing information from the files stored on the computer. Ideally, both a firewall and anti-virus software should be used so that your PC is protected from both types of attack.

The firewall provided with Windows 7 will be included as part of a standard installation and it will be switched on by default. The status of the Firewall can be checked by going to the Windows Control Panel, selecting an icon view, and operating the Windows Firewall link near the bottom of the window. This produces a window like the one shown in Figure 2.25, and in this example the Firewall is switched on. It can be switched on and off via the appropriate link in the left-hand section of the window, but it should only be switched off if a more sophisticated firewall program has been installed. Having more than one firewall program running at once is more or less guaranteed to produce problems.

There are a number of firewall settings that can be altered via the Advanced Settings link and the dialogue box that this produces. It is not normally necessary to do so, and no changes should be made here unless it is essential in order to get some form of Internet service to work properly. Where appropriate, the Help or Support section of the service's web site should give details of the necessary changes.

Boot failure

In the early days of computer viruses it was quite normal for an infected computer to be rendered unbootable. The nature of malware has changed somewhat over the years, and it is now quite rare for malicious software to render a computer unable to boot into Windows. Rather than rendering you computer useless, the attackers need it to be in working order so that they can exploit it in some way. Unfortunately, there are still malicious programs that, once ensconced in your PC, will set about damaging the operating system so that it will no longer function well enough to complete the boot process.

It can be very difficult to sort things out once the computer has reached the stage where Windows will no longer run. Antivirus software is mostly dependent on Windows running reasonably well, and is therefore unusable unless the computer can be booted into Windows, and will function properly for some time thereafter. Without Windows it is not

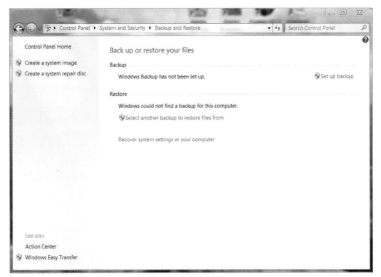

Fig.2.26 The Backup and Restore section of the Control Panel

possible to go online for help, most diagnostic software will not run, manual changes to the system are not possible, and most avenues become closed.

There are two approaches to returning the computer to normality once a virus or other malware has rendered it unbootable. Ideally the hard disc drive should be reformatted and Windows should be installed from scratch. In addition to getting Windows working again, this should ensure that the infection is removed from the hard disc drive. With Windows operating again, it is then a matter of installing the applications programs and restoring the data files.

Of course, this method is reliant on all your data files being backed up, since reformatting the hard disc drive effectively wipes any data files it contains as effectively as it removes the virus. It is essential to have backup copies of any important data so that you are not "caught short" if disaster strikes. Bear in mind that a virus might damage or delete data files as well as system files. Repairing the system and making Windows bootable again will not necessarily leave the computer as it was before the attack, complete with all your data files. Also bear in mind that a hard disc failure could destroy your data files, or make it necessary to use an expensive data recovery service in order to retrieve them.

Fig.2.27 Select the correct drive

The second approach is to attempt to repair the damaged system and make it bootable again so that an antivirus program can be used to search for and eliminate the infection. This requires some form of bootable rescue CD-ROM or DVD. Some antivirus programs are supplied with a bootable rescue disc or set of discs, and some others have a facility for making a rescue disc. There is no guarantee that a facility of this type will remove the infection, or that it will make the system bootable again. However, if you have something of this type it makes sense to try it. The computer might be quickly returned to normality, and it is unlikely to be any worse than it was before.

Windows has a repair facility that can be accessed by booting into the Windows installation disc. It is still possible to use this facility if you have a preinstalled version of Windows that does not include an installation disc, but you must make a system repair disc. The completed disc contains a little less than 150 megabytes of data, so either a CD writer or DVD type can be used to make the disc.

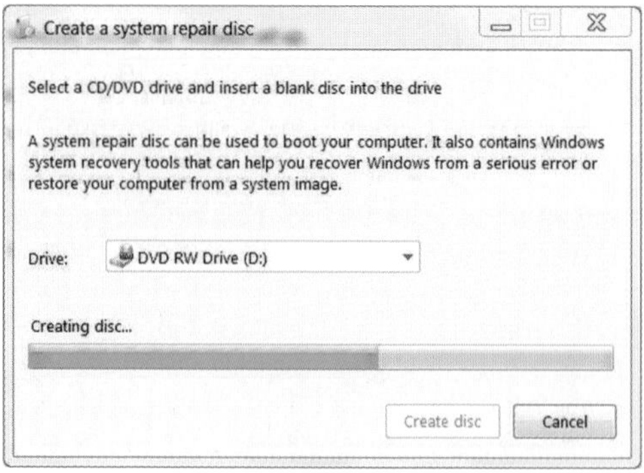

To make a system repair disc it is first a matter of going to the normal version of the Windows Control Panel. In the System and Security section, operate the "Back up your computer" link. This produces the window of Figure 2.26, where the

Fig.2.28 The rescue disc is being created

"Create a system repair disc" link in the left-hand panel is activated. If there is more than one suitable drive, use the pop-up window of Figure 2.27 to select the correct one, and then operate the Create Disc button. A bargraph will then appear at the bottom of the window (Figure 2.28) to indicate how things are progressing, and with most drives it will only take a minute or two to produce the disc.

Backup

Ideally there should be a complete backup of the hard disc drive, plus a further backup file containing any new data since the full backup was made. A full backup should be an image file. In other words, it should not simply be a copy of all the files on the hard disc drive, but it should also include the information required in order to store everything on the hard disc in its original position. With the contents of the disc restored using an image file, the disc should be exactly as it was when the backup was made. It should boot into Windows and operate as it did originally, the application programs should be installed and working, with any customisation still in place, and the data files should all be present.

A complete backup of this type is not practical as a way of backing up data at the end of each day or the end of each session with the computer. It takes too long and could increase the wear on the disc drives sufficiently to greatly shorten their operating lives. The normal approach to the problem is to make an initial backup of the complete system, but to only do so again if a large change is made to the system. For example, it might be worthwhile making a new backup after installing one or two major items of software and carrying out any required customisation.

A separate backup is made of data files, and this can be done on a daily basis, or even more frequently if required, since relatively little needs to be copied. With this method there is no need to copy system or program files each time a backup is made, and it is not even necessary to copy data files that have not been altered since the previous backup was made. It is just a matter of copying any files that have been edited since the previous backup was produced, and copying any new files as well.

Windows 7 backup

I think it is fair to say that the built-in backup and restore features of Windows have not really been one of its strong points in the past. Matters improved somewhat with Windows Vista, and they are even better with Windows 7. Unlike previous versions, you get some quite sophisticated backup and restore facilities even if you do not have one of the more expensive editions such as Windows 7 Ultimate. The built-in backup and restore facilities of both Home editions of Windows 7 are all most users will ever need.

Windows 7 includes both types of backup and restore facility, so one of these can be used to create an image of the boot disc. The disc image is restored using the facilities available from the Windows 7 installation disc, or from the system rescue disc described previously. The backup and restore features are therefore fully usable even if a Windows installation disc was not included when you purchased your PC. However, it is essential to make a system rescue disc if you wish to use this facility and do not have an installation disc.

In order to create a backup of the entire system, first go to the Backup and Restore section of the Control Panel (Figure 2.26), and then activate the "Create a system image" link near the top left-hand corner of the Window. This launches a new window (Figure 2.29), but there will be a short delay while Windows searches for suitable backup drives. Obviously the amount of storage space required for a complete backup depends on the number of installed programs and the amount of data stored on the hard disc drive. Even if the backup is made before large amounts of data start to accumulate on the hard disc, something in the region of 100 gigabytes of storage space could be needed.

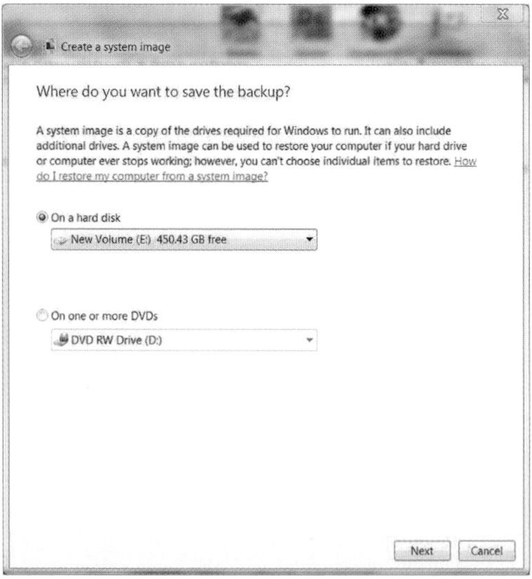

Fig.2.29 Select the correct backup drive

Most types of storage, including CD-R discs, are not really a practical proposition when such large amounts of storage are involved. Writable DVD discs are more practical, but about twenty of these discs might be needed. Making the backup could be quite time consuming, and the discs would cost several pounds. However, it is definitely a good idea to use DVDs in cases where no other suitable backup drive is available. The time and money spent on making the backup will seem well worth it if the system becomes seriously damaged and has to be reinstalled from scratch.

The best type of backup storage is a hard disc drive, which can either be an external USB type of a second internal drive. An external drive is generally regarded as the better option, presumably because it can be physically separated from the rest of the computer, and need not even be kept in the same building as the rest of the computer system. If anything should happen to the computer, there is a good chance that the backup drive and files will not be damaged. This is also an advantage when using DVDs to store the backup files, since the DVDs can be stored well away from the computer, and should be.

A second internal hard drive is more convenient than the other methods, but has to be regarded as slightly less secure. A big advantage of a hard disc drive, whether internal or external, is that there is no need to keep feeding the drive new discs when making a backup. With DVDs you have to stay with the computer while the backup is made, perhaps changing discs about twenty times before the task is completed. With a hard disc drive you just start the backup process and leave the computer to get on with it. The process is likely to be much quicker when using a hard disc drive. This is partially due to the lack of delays while swapping discs, but is mainly due to the fact that hard disc drives can read and write data at a faster rate than DVD drives.

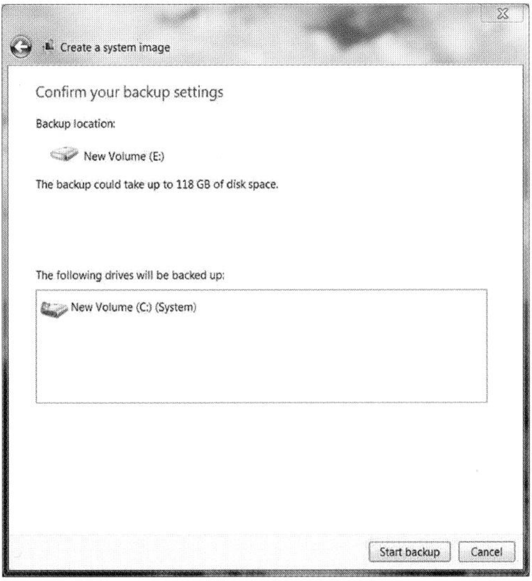

In this example there is a choice of an internal hard disc drive or a DVD type, and I opted to use the

Fig.2.30 Confirm the backup settings

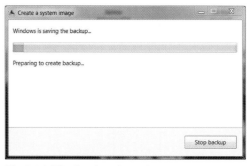

Fig.2.31 The backup is under way

internal hard disc. The next window (Figure 2.30) shows the selected drive, and the drive that will be backed up. The latter is whichever drive contains the Windows installation, and it is normally drive C:. The maximum size of the backup file is given, but there is no estimation of the time that it will take to complete the process. Practical experience suggests that it usually takes minutes rather than hours when using a hard disc drive as the backup device. However, it could take an hour or more when using DVDs, or if a very large backup file will be produced.

If everything is as it should be, start the backup process. A small pop-up window will show how things are progressing (Figure 2.31). When backing up to a DVD drive you will be prompted to change to a new disc every few minutes. The discs should be labelled so that they can be used in the right sequence when restoring the backed-up system. The pop-up message of Figure 2.32 appears when the process has been completed. The message asks if you wish to produce a rescue disc. If you have not already done so and you do not have a Windows installation disc, you should certainly take this opportunity to make a rescue disc. Remember that the backup is useless unless you have either a Windows installation disc or a rescue type.

Fig.2.32 The backup has been completed

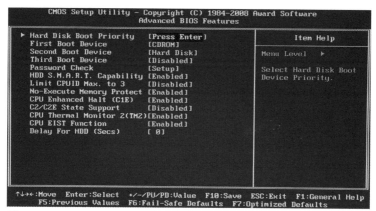

```
     CMOS Setup Utility - Copyright (C) 1984-2008 Award Software
                        Advanced BIOS Features
 ┌─────────────────────────────────────────┬──────────────────────────┐
 │ ► Hard Disk Boot Priority   [Press Enter] │       Item Help          │
 │   First Boot Device         [CDROM]       │                          │
 │   Second Boot Device        [Hard Disk]   │  Menu Level    ►         │
 │   Third Boot Device         [Disabled]    │                          │
 │   Password Check            [Setup]       │  Select Hard Disk Boot   │
 │   HDD S.M.A.R.T. Capability [Enabled]     │  Device Priority.        │
 │   Limit CPUID Max. to 3     [Disabled]    │                          │
 │   No-Execute Memory Protect [Enabled]     │                          │
 │   CPU Enhanced Halt (C1E)   [Enabled]     │                          │
 │   C2/C2E State Support      [Disabled]    │                          │
 │   CPU Thermal Monitor 2(TM2)[Enabled]     │                          │
 │   CPU EIST Function         [Enabled]     │                          │
 │   Delay For HDD (Secs)      [ 0]          │                          │
 │                                           │                          │
 │                                           │                          │
 ├─────────────────────────────────────────┴──────────────────────────┤
 │↑↓→←:Move  Enter:Select  +/-/PU/PD:Value  F10:Save  ESC:Exit  F1:General Help │
 │    F5:Previous Values  F6:Fail-Safe Defaults  F7:Optimized Defaults  │
 └─────────────────────────────────────────────────────────────────────┘
```

Fig.2.33 The BIOS Setup program can be used to alter the boot disc
priority

Restoring

Restoring a system backup is fairly straightforward, but it is not done
from within Windows. Instead, the computer is booted from either a
rescue disc or a Windows installation DVD. The facilities provided by
the boot CD or DVD are then used to restore the backup. The computer's
BIOS must be set to boot from the DVD drive before it tries to boot from
the hard disc. It is unlikely that the computer will attempt to boot from
the DVD drive if the priorities are the other way around, and it will certainly
not do so unless the DVD drive is set as one of the boot devices.

It is quite likely that the computer will already be set to boot from the
DVD drive. If this is the case, a message will probably appear on the
screen indicating that any key must be operated in order to boot from
the DVD drive. This message appears quite briefly, so be ready to press
one of the keys. The computer will try to boot from the hard disc if you
"miss the boat". It will then be necessary to restart the computer and try
again.

It the computer will not boot from the DVD drive it is likely that it is not set
as the first boot drive, and this must be corrected by entering the BIOS
Setup program. The exact way in which this is done varies from one
BIOS producer to another, but it usually just involves pressing a certain
key when the computer is going through its testing procedure just after
switch-on. It is usually the Delete or Escape key that has to be operated,
but it is the F2 function on my Dell PC, and there are other variations.

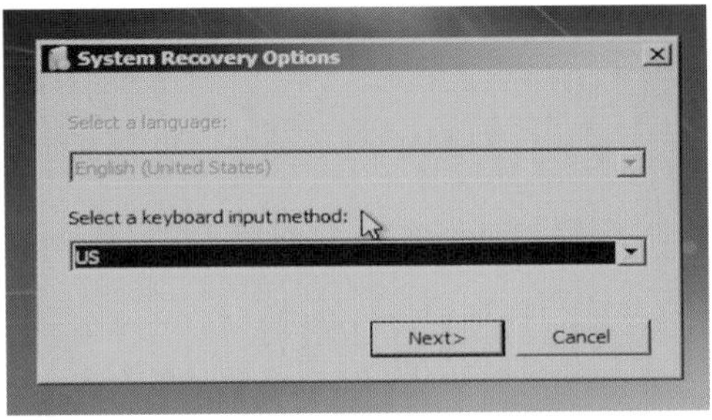

There will usually be an onscreen message that tells you which key to press. Failing that, the instruction manual for the computer should provide this information.

Fig.2.34 Select the right keyboard language

Once into the Setup program it is a matter of finding the section that deals with the boot order, and then setting the DVD drive as the first boot disc, and the hard disc drive as the second boot disc. On my Dell PC it is the Advanced BIOS Settings section that is required (Figure 2.33). Do not be tempted to change any other settings as doing so could prevent the computer from operating properly. Once the required changes have been made it is just a matter of saving the changes and exiting the BIOS Setup program.

If the computer still refuses to boot from the DVD drive it is possible that the BIOS is ignoring the keyboard. This sometimes happens with USB keyboards, and the solution is to go back into the BIOS Setup program and find the section that deals with support for USB devices. Make sure that USB keyboard support is enabled. It should then be possible to boot from the DVD drive.

The restoration process using a rescue disc is similar to the one used with a Windows installation disc, but they are not quite the same. First we will consider the process using a rescue disc. After various files have been loaded from the DVD, things should come to a halt with the screen of Figure 2.34. Use the drop-down menu to select the appropriate keyboard language and then operate the Next button.

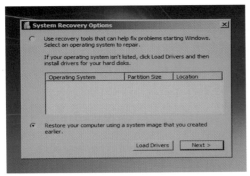

Fig.2.35 No Windows installation has been detected

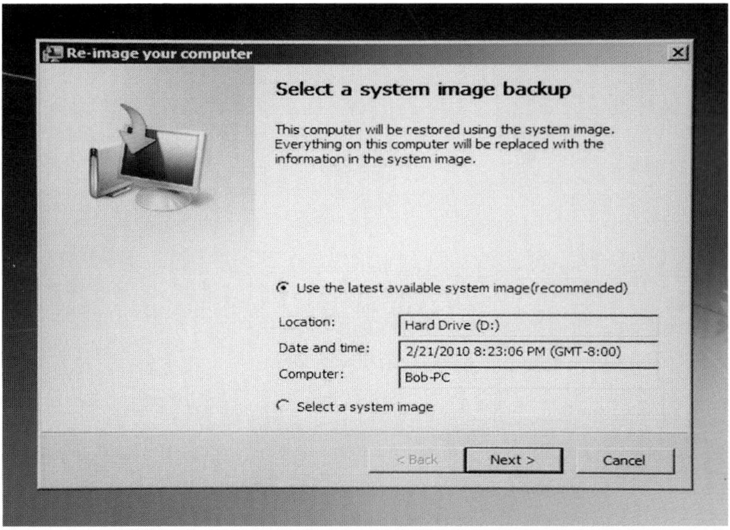

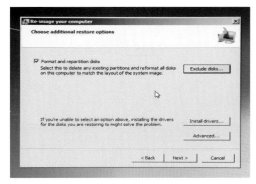

Fig.2.36 *The last backup is used by default, but a different one can be chosen*

This produces a window that will show any Windows installations that have been detected. In the example of Figure 2.35 the Windows installation was too badly damaged to be detected, and the main panel is therefore blank. In the current context it does not matter whether the existing installation is detected, since the current installation is being replaced rather than repaired. The radio buttons give the choice of using recovery tools or restoring a backup, and it is obviously the second option that is needed here. The

Fig.2.37 *The disc can be repartitioned*

next window (Figure 2.36) allows a backup to be selected, but the default setting is to use the latest one that is available. This window will appear

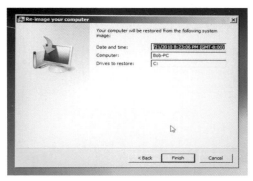

Fig.2.38 *A summary of the selected options*

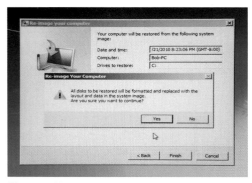

Fig.2.39 *You are warned that all data on the disc will be lost*

even if there is only one backup available. Unless there is a good reason for doing otherwise, just accept the default setting.

The next window (Figure 2.37) gives the option of repartitioning and formatting the hard disc drive, which deletes any existing contents of the disc. It is probably best to use this option, and it should certainly be used when the hard disc is infected with some form of malware. Repartitioning and formatting the disc should remove all its contents, including the infection. By default all the discs will be repartitioned and formatted, apart from the one that contains the backup files of course. There is the option of excluding specified discs, and it is as well to use this option to check that you are not about to obliterate something important. Has some form of removable disc been left in its drive for example?

A summary of the selected options is provided at the next window (Figure 2.38), and then a warning message appears, explain that all

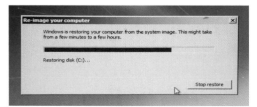

Fig.2.40 *The backup is under way*

existing data will be erased from the discs that are being restored (Figure 2.39). Operating the Yes button starts the restoration process, and there is the usual pop-up window to show how

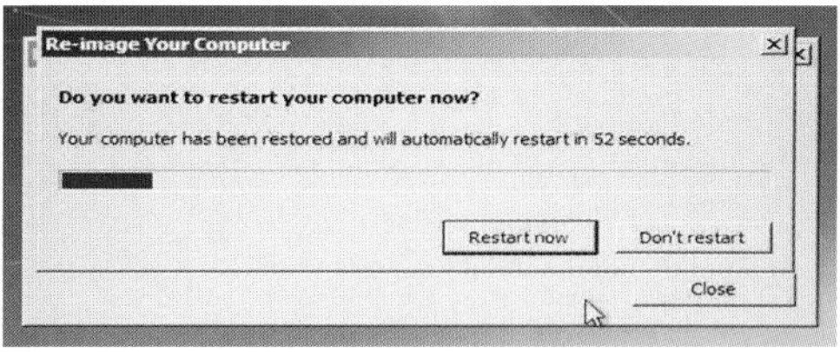

Fig.2.41 The computer will restart itself

matters are progressing (Figure 2.40). Eventually the process will be completed and the message of Figure 2.41 will appear. The computer should be restarted and it should boot into Windows, with the restored drives exactly as they were when the backup was made.

windows is loading files...

Fig.2.42 There will be a delay while various files are loaded

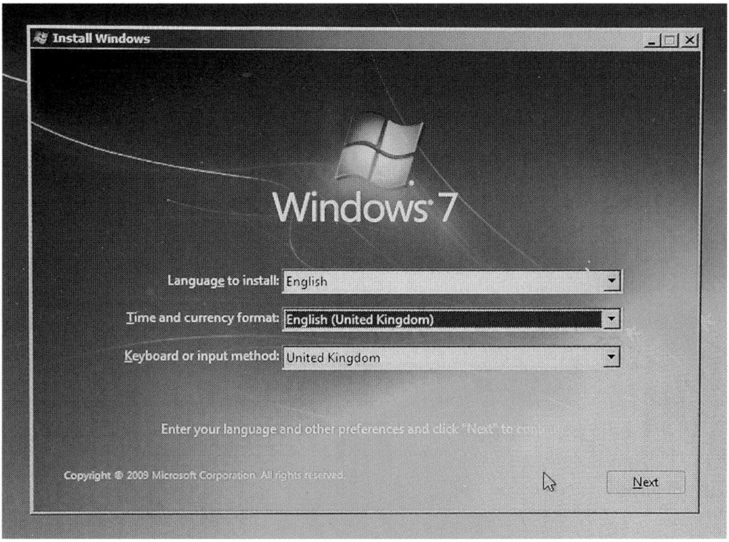

Fig.2.43 Select the required language options using the three menus

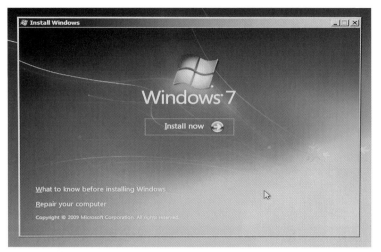

Fig.2.44 Operate the "Repair your computer" link

Installation disc

In order to use the restoration feature of a Windows 7 installation disc it is again a matter of booting from the disc, and the message of Figure 2.42 will be shown at the bottom of the screen while various files are loaded. The window of Figure 2.43 will then appear, and the three menus are used to select the correct language options. Operate the "Repair your computer" link at the next window (Figure 2.44), and there will then be a delay while the program searches

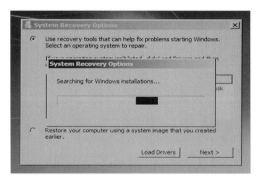

Fig.2.45 A search is made for Windows installations

for Windows installations (Figure 2.45). When the search is finished, opt to restore a backup at the window of Figure 2.46. At the next window

(Figure 2.47) you can select a backup or use the latest one that is available, and the process then continues as before.

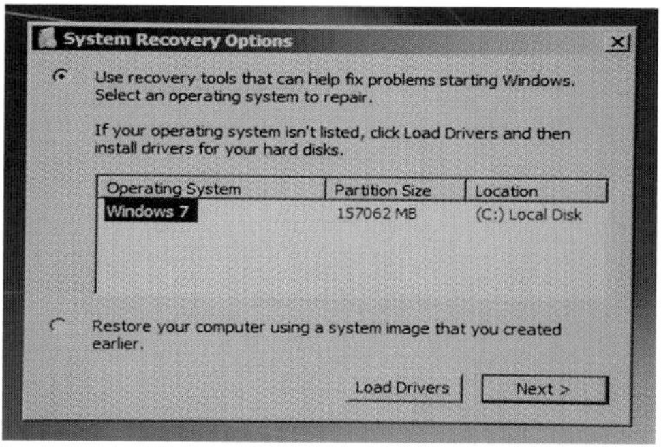

File backup

It is not essential to use a backup utility to produce backup copies of your data files. The system

Fig.2.46 Opt to restore a backup

used by many, including myself, is to first make a system image using the Windows facility described previously, and to then make backup copies of data files as they are produced. This does not take much time, and it largely eliminates the risk of losing any data. If disaster should strike, getting things back to the way they were before the catastrophe could well take under an hour.

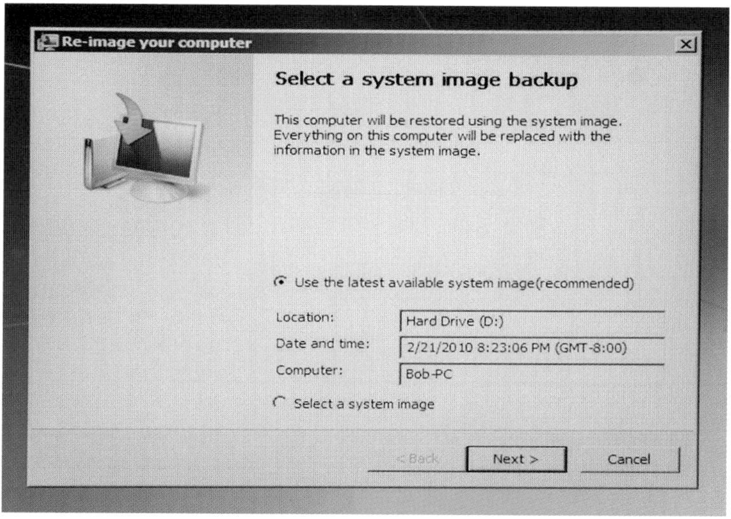

Fig.2.47 Choose a backup or accept the default (the last one made)

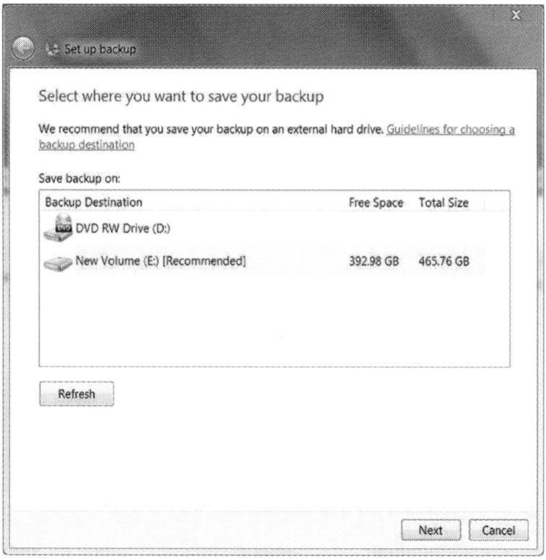

Fig.2.48 The available drives are shown

If the automated approach is preferred, Windows has a built-in system for backing up data files, and this can be set to automatically copy any new files and files that have been altered since the last backup was made. It is set to operate at a certain time every day, week, or month. Backing up on a monthly or weekly basis is only a practical proposition if the computer will be used to produce small amounts of data that are of relatively little importance. Even with a daily update it is possible to lose a whole day's work if the system goes haywire at just the wrong time.

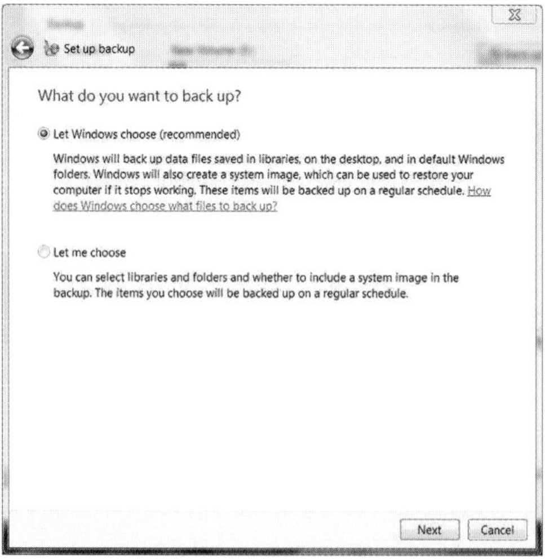

Fig.2.49 You can opt to choose the data files

It is not essential to use automated backing up, and there is also the option of producing new backups on demand. This is probably the more practical approach when new data is generated sporadically rather than on a regular basis. Note that it is still possible to produce backups on demand even if the automatic facility has been switched on.

A simple setting-up procedure has to be completed before the file backup facility can be used, even if you will only use the on demand part of this facility. From the Backup and Restore section of the Control Panel (Figure 2.26), operate the "Set up backup" link. This will launch a new window, and after a brief scan of the system you will be shown the available drives (Figure 2.48). Left-click the entry for the

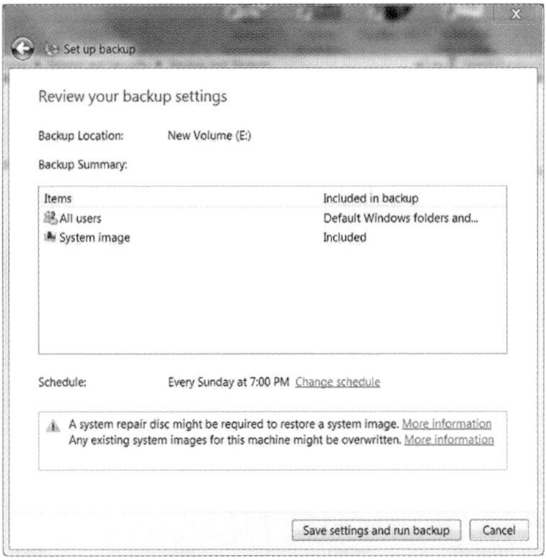

Fig.2.50 The selected options are shown here

drive you wish to use, and then operate the Next button.

You then have a choice of letting Windows choose the files that will be backed up, or choosing the folders yourself. (Figure 2.49) The important

point to bear in mind here is that Windows will only back up data files stored in the standard locations unless it is told to do otherwise. In other words, files in locations such as a folder on the desktop or in Documents or Music folders will be backed up, but files in a folder you have created on one of the drives will not. Therefore, if you let Windows choose which folders to back

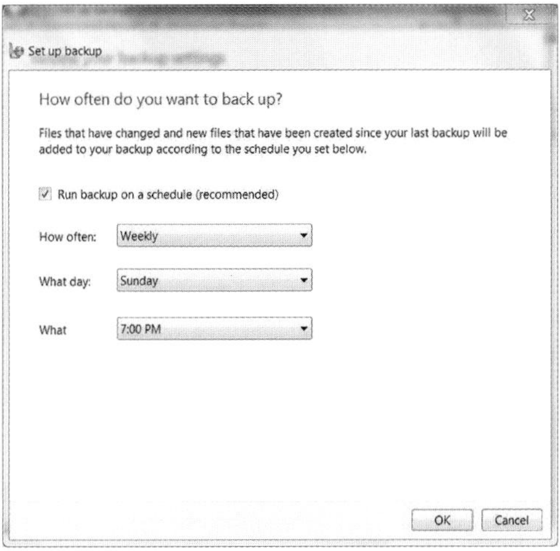

Fig.2.51 Set the backup the schedule here

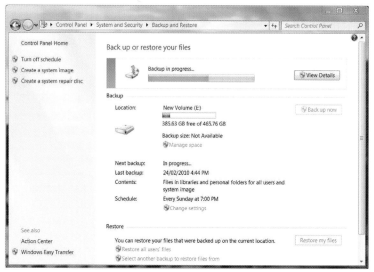

Fig.2.52 A manually initiated backup is under way

up it is essential to store your data folders in Windows approved fashion and not simply scatter them all over the hard disc drive.

If you prefer to "do your own thing", it is essential to use the option that lets you specify the folders to be backed up. It is also essential to keep the settings in the backup program up-to-date if new folders containing data files are added to the system. There is otherwise a risk that some folders containing data files will be ignored by the backup program. Being realistic about matters, it is probably safer to stick to the standard Windows folders if you intend to use this backup facility.

The next window (Figure 2.50) simply confirms the actions that have been selected. Note that it is not necessary to make a system image prior to using this backup program, since an image file will be produced the first time the program is run. In the following window (Figure 2.51) the required backup schedule is selected using the three drop-down menus. Remove the tick from the checkbox if scheduled backups are not required. That completes the setting up process, but no backup will be produced at this stage. An automatic backup will be produced at the appropriate time if scheduling has been selected, or the process can be started manually by going to the Backup and Restore section of the Control panel and operating the "Back up now" button (Figure 2.52).

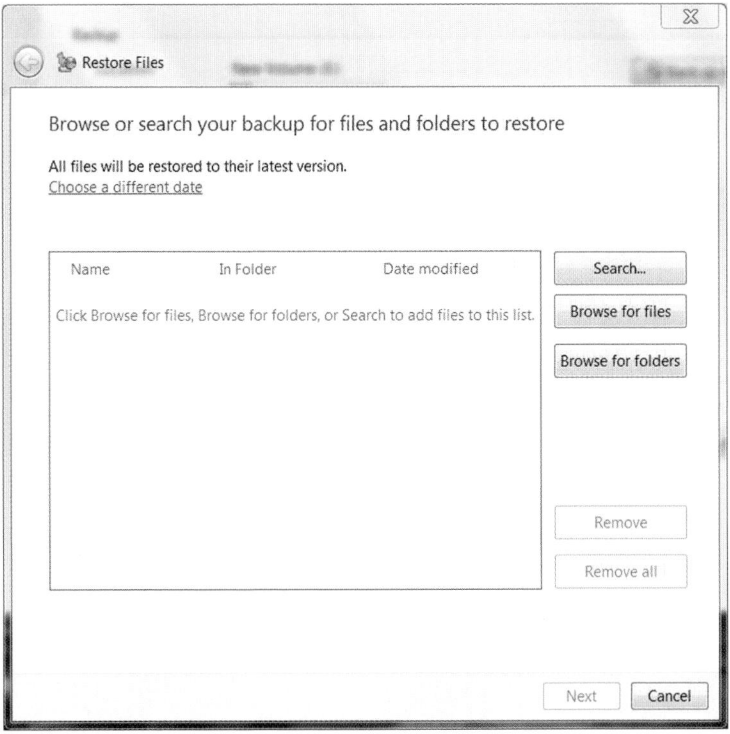

Fig.2.53 You can opt to browse for folders or for files

Restoring files

Files are restored from within Windows, so where appropriate, the system image must be restored first so that the computer can be booted into Windows. It is then a matter of going to the Backup and Restore section of the Control Panel and operating the "Restore all users' files" link if you wish to restore all the data files that have been backed up.

It is not essential to restore all the files, and it is possible to select individual folders or even individual files for restoration. Selective restoration is achieved by operating the "Restore my files" button, which produces the window of Figure 2.53. This enables the user to browse for folders or for files (Figure 2.54), and there is also a standard Windows search facility available here.

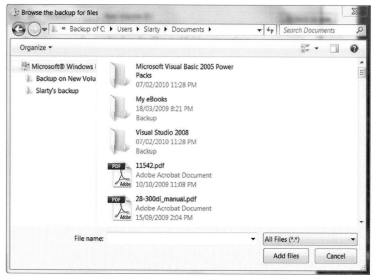

Fig.2.54   If required, it is possible locate and restore individual files in the backup. Note that this is not possible with a system image backup

Troubleshooting

Software compatibility

As pointed out in Chapter 1, where an old program gives problems with Windows 7 it is possible to set the operating system to give a higher degree of compatibility. This is achieved using a compatibility mode. This should not be regarded as the normal way of dealing with a software compatibility issue. The best way to solve a problem of this type is to go to the software manufacturer's web site to search for a software patch that will make the software fully compatible with Windows 7. In some cases it might be necessary to upgrade to the current version of the software. Only use a compatibility mode if a Windows 7 compatible version cannot be obtained.

It has to be emphasised that it is not a good idea to use a compatibility mode with utility software, or any programs that produce an incompatibly warning message when upgrading to Windows 7. Ignoring warnings is likely to cause damage to the operating system, and is unlikely to get

the troublesome software working properly. The idea of this facility is to make Windows 7 more accommodating to old programs that take shortcuts that are not normally permitted under this version of the operating system. It is of no use with a utility program that is specifically designed for an earlier version

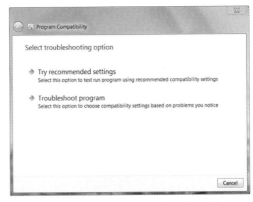

Fig.3.1 Try the recommended settings first

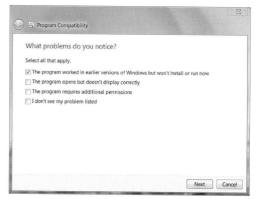

Fig.3.2 Select the required options in standard wizard fashion

of Windows and will try to hack into Windows 7 as if it was that earlier version.

One way of altering the compatibility of a program is to find the program file using Windows Explorer, and the right-click its entry. Alternatively, right-click a desktop shortcut or the menu entry used to launch the program. With either method, choose the "Troubleshoot compatibility" option in the pop-up menu. There will be a short delay while Windows checks for compatibility issues, and then the window of Figure 3.1 will appear on the screen. Initially it is best to use the option that applies the recommended settings. If this fails to cure the problem you can then try again and use the "Troubleshoot program" option. This starts a wizard (Figure 3.2), and it is then just a matter of selecting the appropriate options until all the required settings have been selected.

The compatibility level can be adjusted manually by right-clicking on a shortcut to the program, or on the entry of the program file in Windows Explorer, and then selecting the Properties option. Using either method, a small window will pop up on the screen. The tabs at the top of the window vary somewhat depending on the exact nature of the program file. Left-clicking the Compatibility tab produces a window like the one shown in Figure 3.3. The middle section of the window has checkboxes that can be used to limit the program to basic video modes.

In most cases it is the upper section that is needed, and the first step is to tick the checkbox marked "Run this program in compatibility mode for". This activates the menu that enables the program to be run in modes that give compatibility with earlier 32-bit versions of Windows. If the program had previously worked perfectly under Windows ME for example, the Windows 98/ME option would be used. Note that it is only necessary to set the level of compatibility once. The correct mode will then be used each time the program is run.

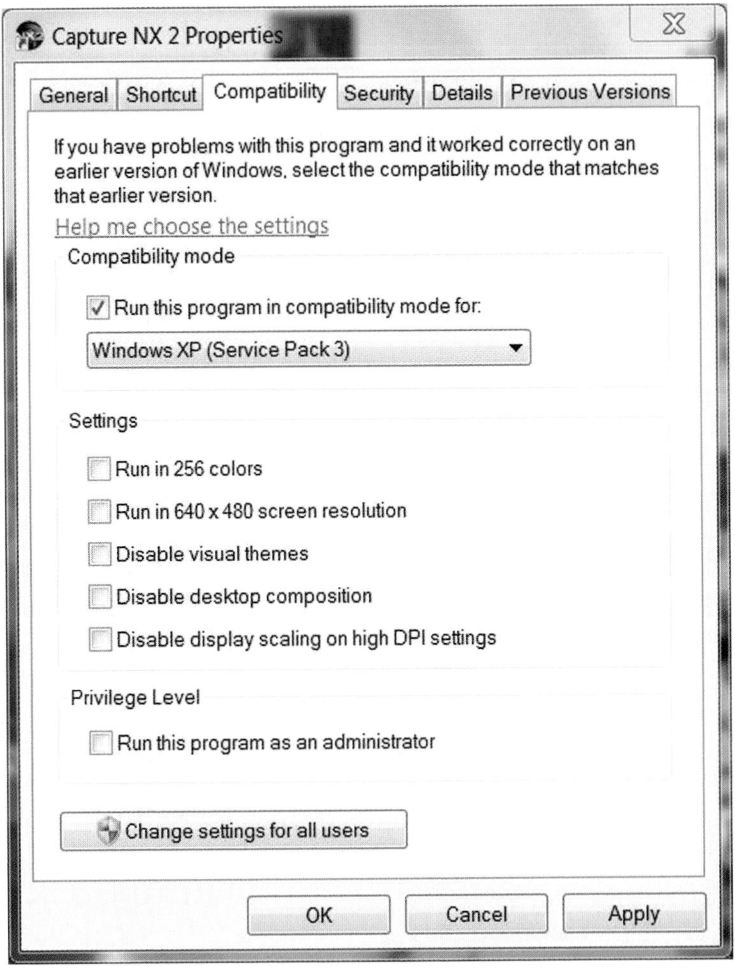

Fig.3.3 The Compatibility section of the program's properties window

System Restore

This is one of the best troubleshooting facilities available when using Windows, and it will often provide a quick and easy solution when the computer has major or minor problems.   The idea of System Restore is to take the operating system back to its state at an earlier date when the

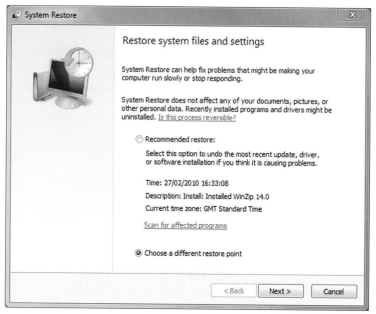

Fig.3.4 The default restoration point can be used or you can select one

PC did boot into Windows and function properly. Clearly it will only work if the computer has been fully operational previously, and it is of no use if you are having problems with a new installation of Windows 7.

There is a System Restore facility available from within Windows, but this is clearly of no use unless the computer can be booted into Windows. However, there are other ways of entering this facility. For the moment, we will assume that it is possible to boot into Windows and launch the System Restore program. This is achieved by going to the Start menu and choosing All Programs, Accessories, System Tools, and System Restore. There might be a delay of a minute or two while the system is scanned, but eventually a window like the one in Figure 3.4 will be launched.

In this example a restoration point is being recommended, and this will usually be the latest one that is available. You can opt to use a different one though, and this is the only course of action if the program does not suggest a restoration point. A window like the one of Figure 3.5 will be produced if you elect to choose a restoration point. Using System Restore should not result in any data files being lost, but taking Windows back to an earlier state can result in recently installed programs being uninstalled.

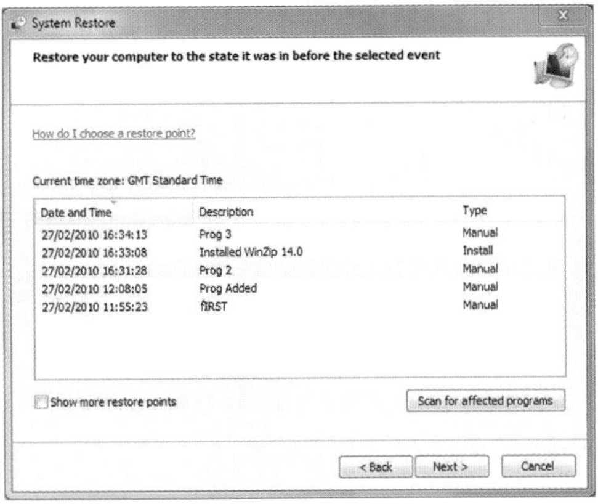

Of course, it could be that the problem was caused by installing a program, and its removal could be an essential part of getting the system working properly again. Even if a program has nothing to do with the problem, it is unlikely to matter too much if it becomes uninstalled. Presumably it can be quickly reinstalled once the system is functioning properly again.

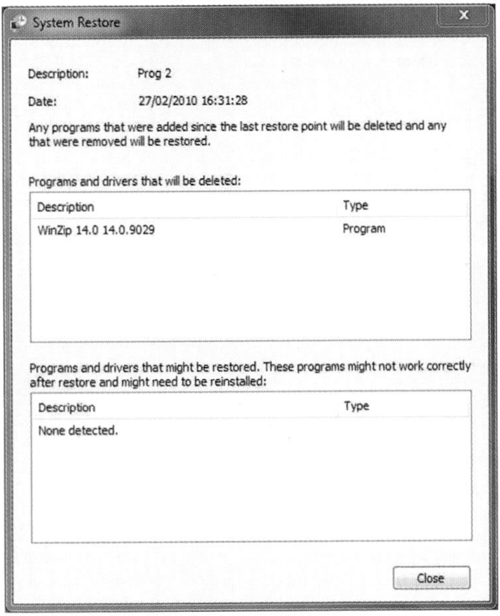

Fig.3.5 Select the required restoration point

Anyway, it is possible to check to see if any programs will be affected by a given restoration point. It is just a matter of left-clicking the entry for the appropriate point and operating the "Scan for affected programs" button. There will be a delay while the system is scanned, and then the results will be shown (Figure 3.6). The upper panel shows the programs that will effectively be

Fig.3.6 One program will be affected

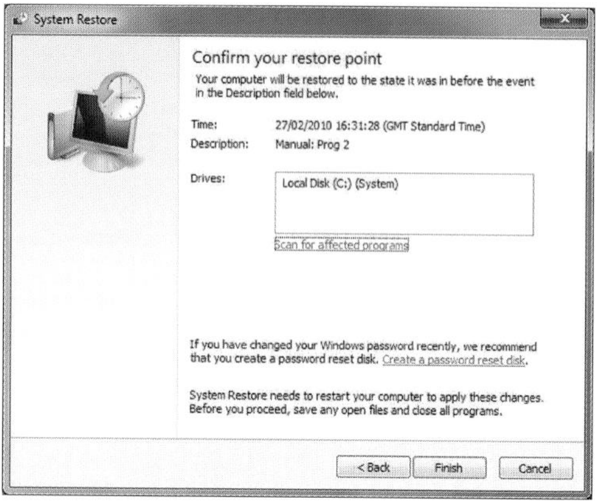

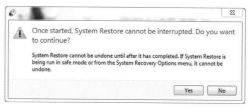

Fig.3.7 Operate the Finish button to use the selected restoration point

Fig.3.8 Do not interrupt the process

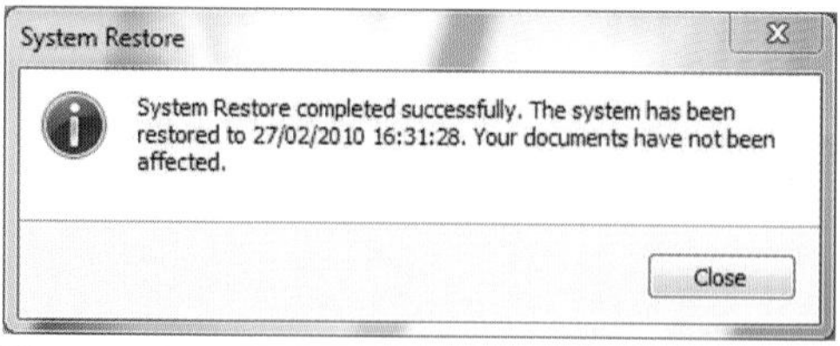

Fig.3.9 The process has been completed successfully

uninstalled, and the lower panel lists any driver software that will have to be reinstalled. In this example only one program is affected. Of course, you will lose any changes made to the Windows settings since the restoration point was made.

After selecting a restoration point you are asked to confirm that the correct settings have been selected (Figure 3.7). The warning message of Figure 3.8 is then produced, and this warns that the restoration process must not be interrupted. Doing so is almost certain to leave the operating system with severe damage, and could possibly leave it in an unrepairable state. It also warns that the restoration is not reversible if this feature is being used with the computer in Safe Mode, or it is being run from an installation or rescue disc.

Opting to go ahead with the restoration process results in a great deal of hard disc activity, a number of onscreen messages, and the computer eventually rebooting into Windows. Once into Windows there should be an onscreen message explaining that the restoration was completed successfully (Figure 3.9). With luck this will have cured the problem and the computer should operate normally.

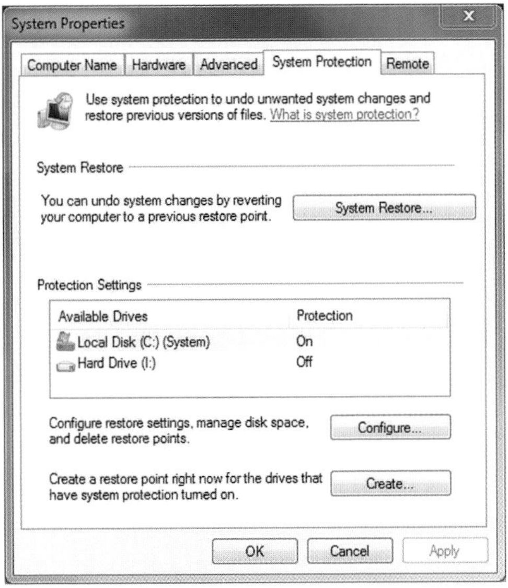

Making a point

Restoration points are produced automatically by Windows from time to time. For example, a restoration point is normally produced

Fig.3.10 The System Protection section of the System Properties window

before any automatic update is installed, and when new application software is installed. This makes it easy to undo a problem that is introduced by an inappropriate update or a piece of "rogue" software. It also helps to ensure that there are plenty of restoration points to choose from if the program becomes unstable for any reason.

You do not have to rely on Windows to produce restoration points, and they can be added manually at any time. A restoration point is added by going to the System Properties window. This can be launched by going to the normal version of the Control Panel and operating the System and Security link. In the new version of the window operate the System link, and in the next version

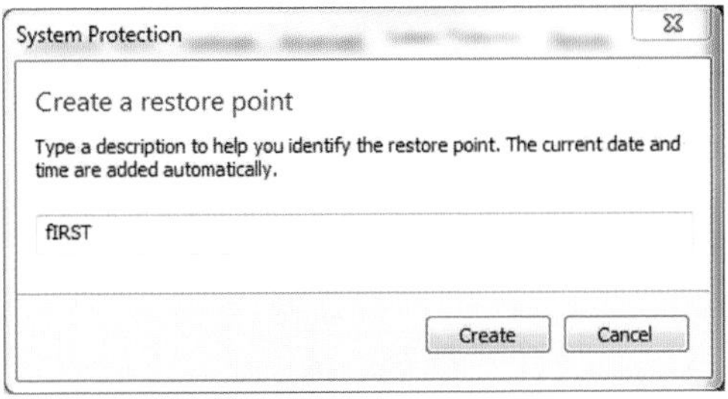

Fig.3.11 The restoration point has been created

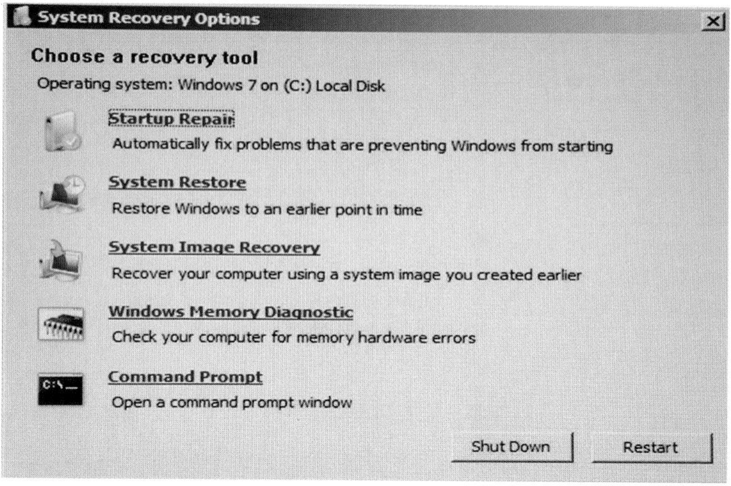

System Recovery Options ☒

Choose a recovery tool

Operating system: Windows 7 on (C:) Local Disk

Startup Repair
Automatically fix problems that are preventing Windows from starting

System Restore
Restore Windows to an earlier point in time

System Image Recovery
Recover your computer using a system image you created earlier

Windows Memory Diagnostic
Check your computer for memory hardware errors

Command Prompt
Open a command prompt window

Shut Down | Restart

Fig.3.12 Several features are available from the Recovery Tools feature

operate the "Advanced system settings" link. This launches the System Properties window, and it is the section under the System Protection tab (Figure 3.10) that is required. Operating the Create button near the bottom of the window generates a new restoration point, and this will be confirmed by a small onscreen message (Figure 3.11).

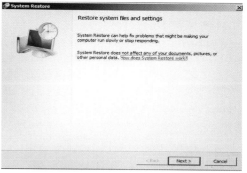

Fig.3.13 The initial window of the System Restore facility

Restore from boot disc

Provided the operating system is still largely intact, it is possible to use a restoration point even if it is not possible to boot into Windows. This feature can be accessed by booting into a Windows installation DVD or a system rescue disc.

When booting from an installation disc, activate the "Repair your computer" link when the screen of Figure 2.44 is reached (refer back to

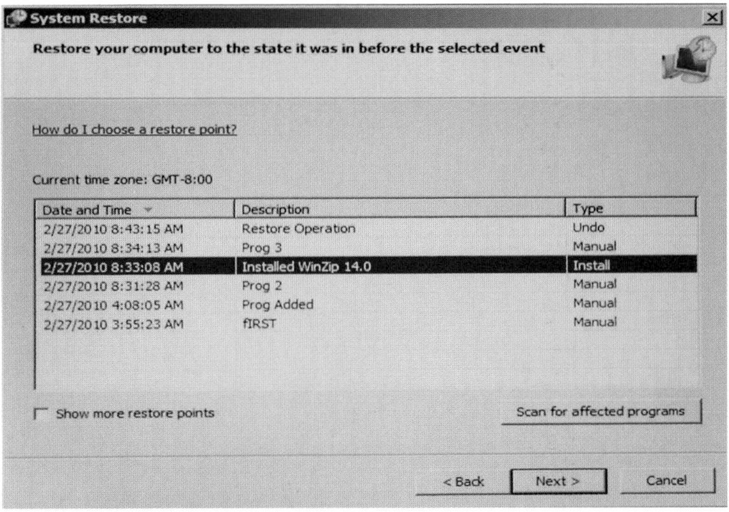

Fig.3.14 Select the required restoration point

Chapter 2). When booting from a rescue disc, opt to use the recovery tools when the window of Figure 2.35 is reached (again, refer back to Chapter 2).

With either method the Recovery Tools window of Figure 3.12 should appear after a short delay while the appropriate files are loaded. From the list of options it is obviously System Restore that is selected, and this option produces the window of Figure 3.13. It is unlikely that a restoration point will be suggested here, and it is really just an information screen. Moving on to the next window (Figure 3.14), here you select the required restoration point. As before, it is possible to select a restoration point and then scan for affected programs and drivers.

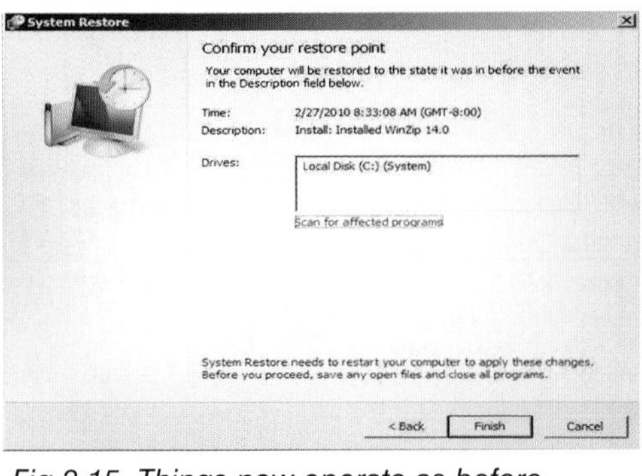

Fig.3.15 Things now operate as before

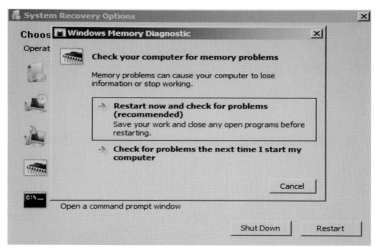

Fig.3.16   The test can be run immediately or when the computer is booted into Windows

Having selected a restoration point, operate the Next button to move on to the next window (Figure 3.15). From here things operate much as they did before, with the selected restoration point being shown. Operating the Finish button brings up a warning message, and operating the Yes button starts the restoration process. Note that this process cannot be reversed when System Restore is run from a rescue or installation disc. The computer will eventually reboot into Windows, and (hopefully) the computer will then operate normally.

Recovery Tools

The are several other options available from the Recovery tools window, and one of these just provides another way of using the restore section of the Backup and Restore facility described in Chapter 2. Another option enables the computer's memory to be tested. This facility tests the computer's main RAM and not any other type of memory, such as video memory, or virtual memory provided by a hard disc drive.

When a problem occurs with a PC running Windows there is perhaps a tendency to assume that it is the operating system that is at fault. This is probably as a result of early versions of Windows producing more than their fair share of problems. Anyway, modern versions of Windows are

```
                        Windows Memory Diagnostics Tool


Windows is checking for memory problems...
This might take several minutes.

Running test pass  1 of  2: 11% complete
Overall test status: 05% complete



Status:
No problems have been detected yet.

Although the test may appear inactive at times, it is still running. Please
wait until testing is complete...

Windows will restart the computer automatically. Test results will be
displayed again after you log on.




  F1=Options                                                      ESC=Exit
```

Fig.3.17 The memory test starts up automatically

more reliable than the ones of ten or more years ago, and it is not safe to assume that the occasional system crash or other error is the result of a flaw in the operating system.

Problems can be caused by hardware glitches, particularly in cases where errors occur in a random fashion rather than when a certain action is carried out. The computer's memory is almost certainly the most common cause of random crashes and errors, but they also can be caused by problems with other parts of the hardware such as the processor or the hard disc drive. Where there is a persistent problem that cannot be definitely connected to the operating system, it is certainly a good idea to try a different tack and make some checks on the computer's hardware.

The pop-up window of Figure 3.16 is produced when the memory test is selected, and this offers the choice of rebooting immediately and running the test, or running it the next time the computer is booted. Either way, once the computer has booted into the test program it will start to run immediately (Figure 3.17). By default it will test the memory twice, and this usually takes a few minutes. If the computer only glitches infrequently it can be worth increasing the number of times the memory is checked. This can be done by repeatedly selecting the memory test, but it is easier to increase the number of passes by operating the F1 function key to bring up the Options screen (Figure 3.18). A useful ploy is to set the

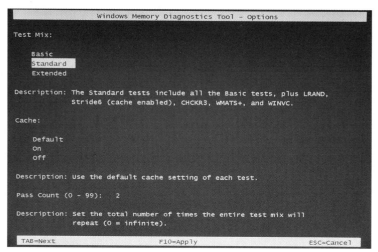

Fig.3.18 The number of passes can be adjusted here

number of passes to zero. The test will then go on repeating itself until you operate the Escape key to bring things to a halt.

A test report will be provided when the computer reboots if a memory error is detected. Memory errors can be caused by inappropriate parameters set in the BIOS Setup program, but it is not advisable to meddle with these settings unless you know exactly what you are doing. The usual cure is to replace the existing memory with a higher quality type. However, in the BIOS Setup program it is usual possible to select a set of fail-safe default settings, and it is worth trying this facility. The parameters used will not squeeze every last ounce of performance from the computer, but they should provide reliable results. If the memory is still unreliable, then it should certainly be replaced.

Startup Repair

The Startup Repair facility is designed to provide a quick fix if the computer will not boot into Windows. It is completely automatic, and it starts to run as soon as this option is selected (Figure 3.19). The computer will reboot into Windows if it repairs the damaged system, but it might reboot into the repair program once or twice first. The message of Figure 3.20 appears if the problem cannot be found and repaired.

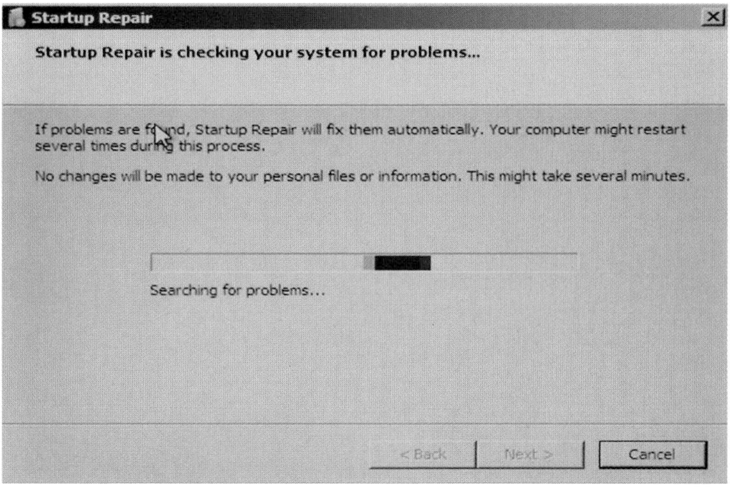

Startup Repair

Startup Repair is checking your system for problems...

If problems are found, Startup Repair will fix them automatically. Your computer might restart several times during this process.

No changes will be made to your personal files or information. This might take several minutes.

Searching for problems...

< Back   Next >   Cancel

Fig.3.19 The Startup Repair facility is completely automatic

Command Prompt

Selecting the Command Prompt option effectively boots the computer into the Windows 7 version of the old MS-DOS operating system. This has a text-only screen where commands have to be typed in (Figure 3.21), and it has its uses for those who have the necessary expertise. It is of limited use otherwise, but removing some of the more awkward viruses and other infections requires the computer to be booted into the

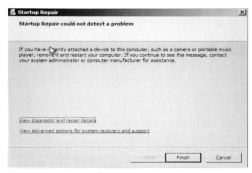

Startup Repair

Startup Repair could not detect a problem

If you have recently attached a device to this computer, such as a camera or portable music player, remove it and restart your computer. If you continue to see this message, contact your system administrator or computer manufacturer for assistance.

View diagnostic and repair details

View advanced options for system recovery and support

< Back   Finish   Cancel

Fig.3.20 No problems were found

command prompt screen so that changes can be made to files, or files can be deleted without interference from the malicious software. However, booting the computer into Safe Mode is usually an easier way of achieving the same thing.

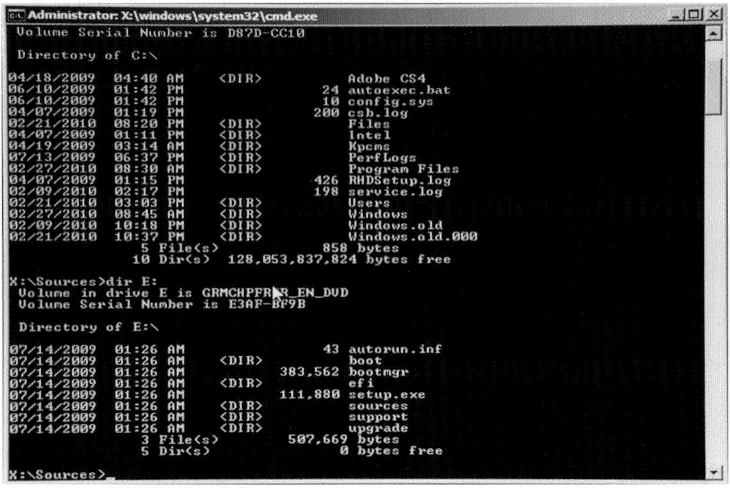

Fig.3.21 The Command Prompt provides an MS-DOS style interface

Using F8

Windows 7 provides various start-up modes that can be useful when the computer refuses to boot properly. In order to boot into one of these modes the F8 function key must be pressed as soon as the BIOS start up routine ends and the boot process begins. There is only a very brief gap between the BIOS finishing its start-up processes and the system starting to boot, so you must press F8 as soon as the BIOS has finished its routine. In fact with some systems the only reliable way of entering Safe mode is to repeatedly press F8 as the end of the start-up routine approaches. Pressing F8 when using Windows 7 brings up the simple menu system shown in Figure 3.22. This is a summary of the options:

Start Windows Normally

Booting using the Normal option takes the PC through a normal Windows boot-up process, but it is obviously of no use if the computer has a major boot problem. Selecting this option will simple result in the computer rebooting and hanging up again. Sometimes Windows "thinks" that it has detected an error during the boot sequence, and it might then go to the Advanced Boot Options screen. If you consider that all is actually well with the system, this option provides a means of trying to boot the computer normally.

```
                        Advanced Boot Options

Choose Advanced Options for: windows 7
(Use the arrow keys to highlight your choice.)

    Repair Your Computer

    Safe Mode
    Safe Mode with Networking
    Safe Mode with Command Prompt

    Enable Boot Logging
    Enable low-resolution video (640x480)
    Last Known Good Configuration (advanced)
    Directory Services Restore Mode
    Debugging Mode
    Disable automatic restart on system failure
    Disable Driver Signature Enforcement

    Start Windows Normally

Description: View a list of system recovery tools you can use to repair
             startup problems, run diagnostics, or restore your system.

  ENTER=Choose                                               ESC=Cancel
```

Fig.3.22 Numerous options are available from this screen

Repair Your Computer

This option simply loads the system recovery tools, as described previously in this chapter.

Safe Mode

Safe Mode boots into Windows 7, but only a minimalist version of the operating system (Figure 3.23). The display is a basic type that used to offer a minimum of 640 by 480 pixel resolution, often together with very limited colour depth. However, with Windows Vista and Windows 7 the resolution will be a minimum of 800 by 600 pixels, and the number of available colours is usually quite reasonable. This mode should be familiar to anyone familiar with troubleshooting on earlier versions of Windows, and it is much the same as the Windows 9x and XP equivalents. In general, the Windows 7 version of Safe Mode is better because less of the hardware is disabled. For example, drives such as CD-ROM and Flash card readers are usually available in the Vista version of Safe Mode, but are often ignored by this mode in earlier versions of Windows. Even with the basic 800 by 600 pixel resolution and the other limitations of this mode, it is often possible to use it to fix Windows problems.

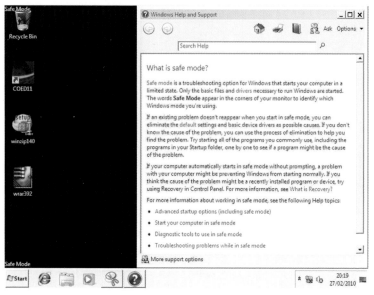

Fig.3.23 A Help window is launched on entering Safe Mode

Although more functional than the Windows 9x Safe Mode, or even the XP version, there are still some items of hardware that do not work in this mode. The soundcard will not be operational, and CD/DVD writers are likely to work as nothing more than simple CD-ROM (read-only) drives. Some hardware drivers are not loaded during the boot process in order to increase the chances of booting into Safe Mode. Any drives that require special drivers are unlikely to be operational in Windows 7's Safe Mode. Peripherals connected to the USB ports do not normally function, but USB keyboards and mice will do so provided the computer's BIOS provides the necessary support. The same is true of most Flash card readers. Startup programs are not loaded when Safe Mode is used.

Many of the usual Windows fault-finding and configuration facilities are available from Safe Mode. In particular, Device Manager and the Registry Editor are both available. Obviously in a minimalist Windows environment there can be some restrictions on services available, but those that are available work more or less normally. Boot problems are often caused by faults in the drivers for new hardware, and having access to Device Manager means that most problems of this type can be rapidly sorted out.

Safe Mode with Networking

This is essentially the same as the normal Safe Mode, but the drivers, etc., needed for Windows networking are loaded. It is possible that network access could be useful because it gives access to shared resources on other PCs, but it is mainly used where the PC is connected to the Internet via a router and some form of broadband connection. By enabling networking, and provided this does not prevent the computer from booting into Safe Mode, the computer will have access to the Internet.

Safe Mode with Command Prompt

Despite the name of this mode, it is nothing like the normal Safe Mode. It would seem to be the same as the Command Prompt mode of the system recovery tools.

Enable Boot Logging

This mode boots the computer normally, but a log file showing the name and status of each driver is placed on the hard disc. The log file is updated as each driver is loaded, and the idea is that the last entry in the file will identify the driver that is causing the system to crash. In practice, things are not quite as simple as that, but it is nevertheless a useful feature if the problem is proving to be elusive.

Enable low-resolution video

The VGA mode is not a normal troubleshooting mode, and it is not intended as an aid to locating faults. It boots the computer normally, but into the standard VGA mode rather than the normal startup mode of the video card. This is useful if there is a problem with the video settings, such as a refresh rate that is too high for the monitor. Boot in this mode and then adjust the video settings to restore proper operation.

Last Known Good Configuration

This mode is similar in concept to using the System Restore facility, but more limited in its scope. It effectively takes the computer back in time to the last settings that enabled it to boot successfully. Unlike the System Restore facility, this mode does not erase or restore files. The file structure remains unchanged, but an earlier version of the Registry is used when booting the computer. Obviously, this mode will only be successful when the cause of the problem is an error or errors in the Registry. The System Restore facility is more likely to restore normal operation.

Fig.3.24 The Action Center has a Troubleshooting link

Directory Services Restore Mode

This mode is probably of no practical value to most users.

Debugging Mode

This is another mode that you will probably never need to use. The computer is booted into Windows kernel mode, and the debugging is then achieved via another computer running a suitable debugger program, with a serial link used to provide communication between the two computers.

Disable automatic restart

Using this mode prevents Windows from automatically rebooting if a system crash occurs. While this could conceivably aid fault diagnosis, leaving the system running in an unstable state could result in damage to system files, or probably any other files on the hard disc drive. This is not a mode that should be used unless you know exactly what you are doing.

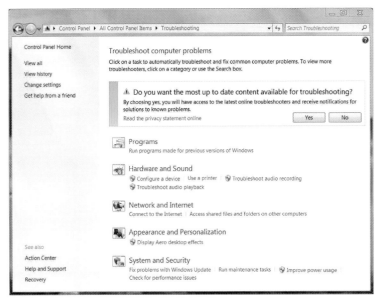

Fig.3.25 Various types of troubleshooting are available here

Disable Driver Signature Enforcement

Drivers that contain an improper signature are loaded when using this mode. I presume that the point of this is to force the system to load a driver that it deems to be unsuitable, but the user considers to be fine, or would like to try anyway.

Action Center

Windows XP has a troubleshooting wizard that can be used to help solve a wide variety of problems. There is no equivalent feature in Windows Vista, and no exact equivalent in Windows 7 either. However, there is a troubleshooting facility available via the Action Center, and this covers a useful range of problems. The Action Center can be accessed by going to the Control Panel, selecting one of the icon views, and double-clicking the Action Center icon. Once into the Action Center (Figure 3.24), activate the Troubleshooting link, which will change the window to the one shown in Figure 3.25.

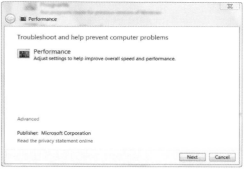

*Fig.3.26 The initial window when checking
for performance issues*

The two buttons near the top of the window are used to opt for the latest troubleshooting content or use only the standard content. It is best to opt for the latest content if the computer has an active Internet connection. There are links to various types of troubleshooting help such as audio devices and other hardware, security, programs, performance issues and Internet connection problems. Sometimes the help is in standard wizard form, while in other cases it is largely automatic. If your computer has a problem in one of the areas covered by this troubleshooting facility, it might provide the quickest and easiest way of sorting things out.

As an example of using a troubleshooter, choosing the "Check for performance issues" produces the window of Figure 3.26, which is really just an information box that briefly explains the purpose of this troubleshooter. This is to check for problems that will not bring the computer to a complete standstill, but might reduce its performance in some way. Operating the Advanced link produces a checkbox, and problems will be automatically repaired if this checkbox is ticked. Operating the Next button starts the checking, and after a few seconds

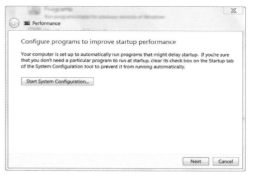

Fig.3.27 The program has a recommendation

the program will either report that it has completed its task, or it will suggest a course of action by the user.

In this case it detected a large number of programs being run automatically at start-up, and it recommended disabling any of these programs that were unnecessary (Figure 3.27). Unless you know what you are doing it is best not to dabble with this type of thing, but if you are sufficiently expert to select the unnecessary programs it is worth trying this feature. Operating the Start System Configuration button launches the System Configuration

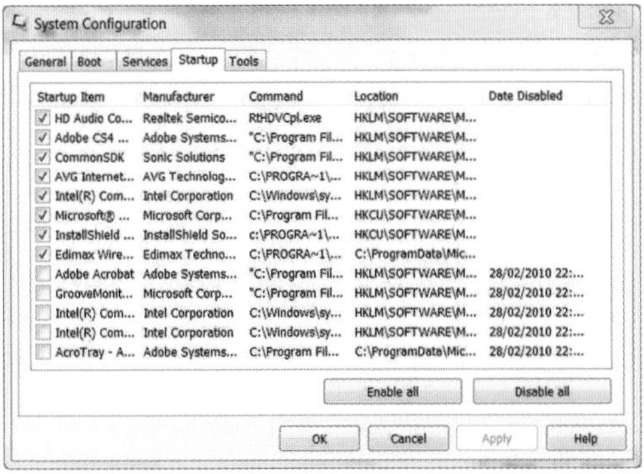

Fig.3.28 Unnecessary programs can be prevented from running at startup

window at the appropriate section (Figure 3.28). Here it is just a matter of unticking the checkbox for any program that you do not wish to run when the operating system starts up.

Disc checking

As pointed out in Chapter 2, erratic operation of a computer is often due to memory or hard disc problems. There is a disc checking facility built into Windows 7, and it is usually possible for this to repair problems with the disc filing system so that the computer can operate normally thereafter. However, this is not to say that it will be possible to recover any damaged data. While it might be possible to recover some fragments of data, the chances of them being of any practical use are very slim. Of course, the disc checking facility cannot make repairs if the problem is in the hardware. It can only confirm that there is a hardware fault.

The disc checking program is easily accessed, and the first step is to go into Windows Explorer. Locate the entry for the drive you wish to check, right-click its entry, and then choose Properties from the pop-up menu. This produces a window that gives some basic information about the drive.

Operate the Tools tab to switch to a Window like the one in Figure 3.29, which includes an error checking facility. Left-clicking the Check Now button produces the small window of Figure 3.30, where two options are available via the checkboxes. The upper checkbox is ticked if you wish to check the filing system, but this check cannot be made while Windows is running. Using this option schedules the check to run the next time the computer is booted into Windows. Using the facilities offered by the lower checkbox is more straightforward. This checks the disc for bad sectors, and using this option results in the disc being checked immediately.

If you opt to have the file system checked, on starting the scan you will instead get a pop-up message that explains the need to provide the scan before the computer boots into Windows. Opt to go ahead anyway, and then you

Fig.3.29 Operate the Check Now button

are then asked if you would like to schedule the scan to be run automatically on the next occasion that the computer is booted into Windows. To go ahead with the checking and fixing process, operate the Yes button and restart the computer. The checking program will be launched during the boot process before the boot drive is left with any open files. The screen will show how things are progressing, and the boot process will continue once the disc checker has completed its task.

Fig.3.30 Two types of scanning are available

Index